Managing MIS Implementation

Management Information Systems, No.1

Gary Dickson, Series Editor

Professor of Management Information Systems
University of Minnesota

Other Titles in This Series

Managing MIS Implementation

by
Lee L. Gremillion

UMI RESEARCH PRESS
Ann Arbor, Michigan

Produced and distributed by
UMI Research Press
an imprint of
University Microfilms International
Ann Arbor, Michigan 48106

Library of Congress Cataloging in Publication Data

Gremillion, Lee L. (Lee Louis)
Managing MIS implementation.

(Management information systems ; no. 1)
Revision of thesis (Ph.D.)—Harvard University, 1979.
Bibliography: p.
Includes index.
1. Business—Data processing. 2. Organizational change.
I. Title. II. Series.

HF5548.2.G72 1982   658'.054   82-4787
ISBN 0-8357-1321-0   AACR2

Contents

Figures

Tables

Acknowledgments

Completion of this study would have not been possible without the active assistance of a large number of individuals. At the risk of inadvertantly omitting some, I will attempt to acknowledge those who contributed.

Primary thanks must go to Professors James L. McKenney, Arthur N. Turner, and Jack R. Buchanan. I am deeply indebted to these individuals for the interest they took in my work, their willingness to divert time for me from their busy schedules, and their many substantive suggestions for the direction of the research. It would be hard to imagine a more interested, helpful, accessible, and congenial group of advisors.

I am also indebted to the many personnel of the United States Forest Service with whom I worked on the project. Literally dozens of USFS personnel at all levels gave generously of their time and interest in assisting me. Particular mention should be made of the help given by Larry Medlock, Region 3 regional Program Analyst. Working with him made the Region 3 experience both highly productive and very enjoyable.

Finally, I would like to express my appreciation to those of my colleagues whose willingness to discuss this research with me was an invaluable aid. Ed Cale, Frank Leonard, and Phil Pyburn in particular often helped by considering some aspect of the research from a fresh point of view.

To each of the individuals named or referred to above, a sincere "thank you" is expressed.

1

Introduction

The changing economics of computing have been widely proclaimed. Industry observers delight in tracing the declining costs of computer hardware, and in projecting that trend into the future (Upton, 1977). Another common display is that of the rising preponderance of personnel costs (as opposed to equipment costs) in the typical data processing budget (Datapro, 1978). All agree, however, that the decreasing cost of computer technology is making that technology available to an ever-widening circle of applications within the organization.

Standing as a constraint to the increased use of the technology, however, is this increasing cost of the personnel required to design systems, write programs, and operate the machines. The equipment itself is getting less expensive, but the people who make the equipment do something useful are getting more expensive. IBM has stated that this factor appears to be the single greatest problem in applying new developments in computer technology to the needs of organizations (Henson, 1977). This can be seen in the example of a decentralized organization which can easily afford to place a time-sharing terminal, or even a minicomputer in each of its units, but cannot afford the man-years of effort it would take to design and program systems for each of those units.

This dilemma is most visible in the case of what is commonly known as "distributed processing" in which actual processing capability (i.e., a central processing unit, or CPU) is put under the control of a subordinate unit. Distributed processing has attracted much attention in the past few years as it has become apparent that there are many instances in which a particular application can be performed for a smaller total hardware cost on several small machines rather than one large machine (Canning, 1973). But hardware costs are only one part of the picture. A savings in hardware expense can be easily offset by increased design and programming costs.

Standardization and control also enter as issues in considering distributed processing. Even if the unit can afford to design and program an individualized system, is it in the overall organization's best interest for them to do so? In many cases it may not be that we can't afford to develop tailored systems for individual units but, rather, that we don't want the units operating individualized systems. If the system itself is intended to be a standardizing mechanism (as in the case of an accounting system, for example) then by definition it cannot be allowed to differ significantly between units. The basic issues of costs, standardization, and control remain, however, whether the case is that of many units with their own minicomputers, or many units sharing a large computer. We still must decide whether we can afford to develop individualized systems for these units, and whether such development would be appropriate even if feasible.

The cost side of the problem is being attacked on several fronts. Efforts are being made on a variety of tools to improve programmer productivity and thus reduce programming costs (Oliver, 1978). The cost advantage of the hardware is being exploited by designing more function into it which makes it easier (i.e., less expensive) to use (Bylinsky, 1975). Computers are even marketed today with the claim that they can be used by persons with no data processing training or experience at all (Datapro, 1976). While these efforts attack the cost problem, they do not address the issues of standardization and control.

Of major potential impact is the increasing use of prewritten, "canned" programs and systems. These are systems which are designed and written at one site and then "plugged in" at multiple other sites with little or no modification. Computer utility packages (sorts, teleprocessing monitors, compilers, etc.) have long been examples of this. Every year this approach becomes more common in the area of application software (Datapro, 1978). Such packages offer an answer in many cases not only to the problem of costs, but also to that of standardization and control.

The approach of "plugging in a package" actually encompasses several realistic scenarios. One such case, as mentioned above, involves purchasing application software from an external source to run on installed hardware. The reasons for taking this approach (as opposed to writing programs from scratch) are typically to reduce expense or to gain the benefits of a "tried and proven" system. In either case, extensive modifications to the system tend to be counterproductive.

Another possibility is that one of a number of organizational subunits has developed a system, and management has decided that other subunits should implement the same system. Again economy and the benefits of a proven system may motivate this approach. In addition, it may be that management wishes to use the system as a means of achieving standardization across the units. A special case of this scenario occurs when management commissions a "pilot" or "prototype" installation of a system. Here the understanding is that a system will be designed, written, tested, and debugged in one (or a few) units and then, once proven, replicated across multiple units. Once this replication process begins, further tailoring of the system must be minimized.

Whatever the scenario, this approach to implementation brings with it the need for a new focus in research on systems development and implementation. As will be shown in the next chapter, previous research has largely concentrated on systems development and implementation as a process of designing and tailoring a system for its potential user. To reap the benefits of installing a standardized system, however, such tailoring must be constrained. Instead, the user must be taught to adapt to the system, altering it as little as possible. How to facilitate this type of implementation is the focus of this study.

As Keen has pointed out in his review of the field (Keen, 1977), two basic deficiencies mark most previous implementation research. The first of these is a lack of a clear-cut definition of when, in fact, a system is "implemented". The second, following from this, is a lack of definition as to what constitutes success in implementation. Is an inventory system implementation considered successful, for example, when the database is built and the computer generates accurate reports; or can it be considered successful only much later when operations personnel rely upon it rather than upon their informal records? Keen describes research which fails to deal with these questions as being in an "undefined setting". In order for the research to be most useful, it must be conducted in a "fully defined" setting, that is, "where the intention of the project is reasonably clear so that the extent to which it meets its aims can be assessed; in this situation, the definition of success is intrinsic and criteria for evaluation apparent" (Keen, 1977). Only when the criteria for success are clear can the research clearly address the critical issues: what factors contribute to success, and what implications can therefore be drawn to guide future implementation activity? From a research point of view, we are saying that we need a clearly measureable dependent variable (success) in order to show relationships between it and any independent variables.

Mandated implementation of a standardized system provides a fully defined setting, and thus an attractive one for implementation research. As explained above, it is an increasingly important situation which merits serious study. More and more, large decentralized organizations are implementing computer-based systems in their subunits through the installation of packages or replication of standard systems. Additionally, implementation and implementation success in such cases are readily defined. Taking the organizational superior's point of view, we say that implementation is the subordinate unit's using the system as it has been ordered. The degree of success is the degree to which actual use is congruent with intended use.

Thus this study addresses the question of how to effectively and efficiently implement a system in an organizational unit, given that the unit's superior desires the implementation and that the system itself is basically fixed. Stated another way, the question is how to help organizations adapt to or learn the system. The objective is to aid the implementation strategist in managing this learning process.

A conceptual scheme or paradigm of system implementation is proposed as an aid in developing this strategy. This is synthesized from previous research, discussions with colleagues, and personal experience. It is intended to provide a framework to help implementation strategists select and design activities which will enhance the likelihood of implementation success. How this might be done, and the structure of the scheme itself, are described in detail in chapter 3.

Chapter 3 also details the research methodology employed by this author. Chapter 4 describes the environment in which the research was conducted; and chapters 5, 6, 7, and 8 contain descriptions and analyses of the field work done and data gathered in conjunction with the research. Chapter 9 draws the overall conclusions of this study.

This study is intended to shed light in the area of directing an organizational change. Research in organizational change is difficult because of the vast number of variables involved (many of which are unmeasureable) and because of the severe constraints on the amount of manipulation the researcher can do. Yet research must be attempted if we are to learn anything about solving these implementation problems which are both real, and, as Keen puts it, "vital to the future of MS/MIS."

2

Background

Computer-based systems can be defined in terms of the Leavitt model of the organization as part of the technology the organization employs (Leavitt, 1964). In this context, the system is a tool used by the persons within the organizational structure to execute a task or tasks.

Systems development, then, is properly concerned with the interfaces between this technological tool and the task(s), structure, and persons in the organization. Successful systems development and implementation is a matter of properly fitting a new piece of technology into the organization.

Looking from this perspective, we can identify three distinct approaches to systems development/implementation theory. One concentrates on the interfaces between technology and the tasks and structure of the organization. Theory of this type involves frameworks for information systems design, or system development process models. The list of examples of contributors to this theory is a long one, and includes Davis (1974), Blumenthal (1974), McFarlan, Nolan, and Norton (1973), Canning (1968), Orlicky (1969), Litecky and Grey (1974), and Benjamin (1971). These all attempt to specify in some detail the tasks and structure of the organization, and then the computer-based tools appropriate to that task and structure. For example, Blumenthal sets out in considerable detail a process for categorizing the tasks the organization performs

Figure 2-1. Leavitt Model of the Organization

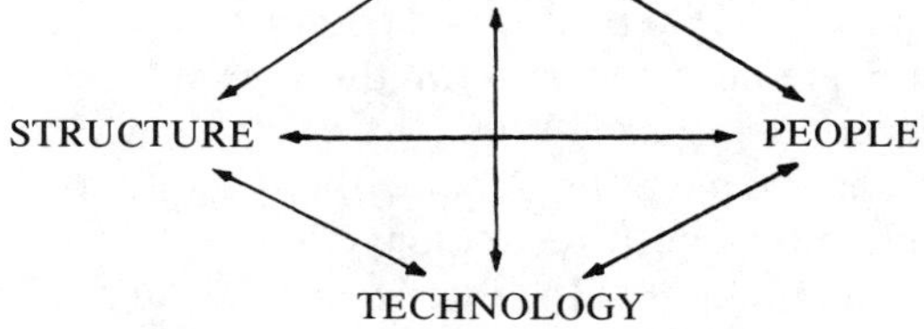

so that the most appropriate one(s) can be selected for computerization first. This might be termed the systems planning approach.

Another approach concentrates on the design of the technological tool itself. This is reflected in the many systems analysis texts (e.g., Cougar (1974), Clifton (1974), or Burch and Strater (1974)), as well as in guidelines for systems development generated internally by many organizations (e.g., Weyerheuser, 1970). These focus on how to build a "well-designed" information system, providing a body of techniques for those designing and implementing systems. This might be termed the systems engineering approach.

MS/MIS implementation research, the third approach, concentrates on the relationships among the technological tools and the persons and structure of the organization. Most work in this area has actually focused on the implementation of operations research/management science (OR/MS) tools (e.g., Huysmans, 1970; Schultz and Slevin, 1975). Much of this has been inspired by a growing awareness on the part of management scientists of an "implementation gap"—that is, a large number of OR/MS models which are developed and never used (Schultz and Slevin, 1975). There is much similarity between implementation of OR/MS models and MIS implementation. In fact, a number of surveys of this literature (e.g., Keen, 1977 and Ginzberg, 1976) treat the two areas as interchangeable. In the past few years the Management Information Systems Research Center at the University of Minnesota has focused specifically on MIS implementations (Narasimham, 1976)).

These various approaches (systems planning, systems engineering, and MS/MIS implementation) are certainly not mutually exclusive. In each case, the overall model is the same; that is, system development and implementation success is a function of the system itself, the organizational structure, the task(s) being performed, and the persons involved. (More precisely, success is a function of the interactions among these factors.) The different approaches, however, concentrate on different subsets of the variables which influence success, and even define implementation slightly differently.

The systems planning approach attempts to answer the question, Given that we know how to computerize things, which things do we computerize? Implementation in this literature generally refers to the entire system selection/development/conversion/operation process. As part of the process of implementing a system, the user's needs are studied and the system patterned to fit those needs.

For the systems engineering school, the question is, Given that we want to apply computer-based technology to a certain task, how do we do it effectively and efficiently? In systems analysis texts, implementation usually has a very specific meaning. Implementation of a system is putting the programs and data on the computer and actually running them in a production mode. For example, Burch and Strater identify system implementation as the step following data file conversion in the overall process of bringing up a computerized application. *i N ool uçiu bJT*

Implementation researchers address the question, How do we get the organization to successfully use these potentially valuable tools which we know how to develop? As Keen points out, there is some disagreement among the various writers in this group as to what exactly constitutes "successful use", or implementation. Huysmans, for example, suggests that there are three "levels of adoption" of a management science model: (1) management action based on the model's solution to the problem, (2) management change caused by the use of the model, and (3) recurring use of the OR/MS approach as a result of satisfaction with this particular model. Keen proposes a fourth level: redefinition of the manager's task as a result of insights gained from using the model.

As Figure 2-2 illustrates, however, the desired end point is really the same in all cases: the "right" system, well-designed and implemented, successfully used by the organization. The difference in the various points of view lies in the variables which each implicitly or explicitly holds constant while addressing its critical variables.

A common thread running through all of these approaches is the idea that implementation success is more likely if the potential user of the system participates in its design. The idea is partially that the user will learn about the system, but, much more importantly, that the designer will be able to tailor the system to fit the user's particular needs. Of course, this assumption is invalidated in the situation we are addressing. One installs prewritten, standardized systems in large part to avoid the expense of tailoring to the user. Additionally, standardized systems are often installed across multiple units precisely to achieve standardization. Thus the prescriptions given in the traditional systems development and implementation literature are fatally flawed from the point of view of our special situation. In fact, the traditional literature often rails against the approach of trying to plug in an already designed system, sometimes referring to this as the "Have tool, will travel" approach. Yet, as we have seen above, there are good reasons for wanting to take such an approach. At times, and these times are becoming more frequent, we simply want to mold the user to the system rather than the other way around.

But how do we effect this? The systems planning literature can help us decide for which applications we should seek computer-based systems, prewritten or otherwise. The systems engineering literature can help us evaluate the intrinsic quality of those packages which are available. The

Figure 2-2.   Hierarchy of Steps to Successful System
              Implementation

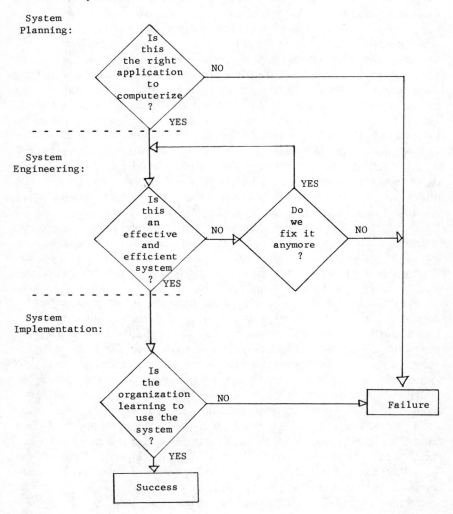

implementation literature can help us be aware of potential implementation concerns as we design and write a system. But there is little research on how to "plug in" the system once it is selected or written. To gain some insight here we must go abroad from the traditional systems development literature.

As McKenney points out, successful implementation of a computer-based system in an organization is basically a manifestation of organizational learning. It involves "a group acquisition of knowledge . . . a behavioral change in an organized human group, and not an individual change" (McKenney, 1978). Implementation involves organizational change, and a directed or planned implementation is a form of planned organizational change.

Traditional planned organizational change research concentrates more on the design of change than on its implementation. Gross, Giaquinta, and Bernstein (1971) surveyed the planned organizational change literature for insights into implementing a planned change in an educational institution. They found that the focus of the literature was on (1) prior factors in the organization or environment which affect receptivity to change, and (2) the change initiation strategy as a factor influencing whether the change was adopted. They concluded that there was little guidance for going from a fixed system we want implemented to specific prescriptions for managing that implementation. *INVOLVE*

Management information systems themselves are, in this traditional literature, a change method. Installing a computer-based system is an example of what Chin and Benne (1975) term the "rational-empirical" change strategy. As they describe it,

> One fundamental assumption underlying these strategies is that men are rational. Another assumption is that men will follow their rational self-interest once this is revealed to them. A change is proposed by some person or group which knows of a situation that is desirable, effective, and in line with the self-interest of the person, group, organization, or community which will be affected by the change. Because the person (or group) is assumed to be rational and moved by self-interest, it is assumed that he (or they) will adopt the proposed change if it can be rationally justified and if it can be shown by the proposer(s) that he (or they) will gain by the change.

By this reasoning the members of an organization should be eager to implement the proposed system once its benefits to the organization have been demonstrated. But reality is not so straightforward. For one thing, demonstrating the desirability of the system to the various members of the organization may be in itself a complex set of tasks. Also, gaining the commitment and cooperation of individuals often requires more than intellectual justification. Just as organizations are complex systems, the requirements for causing them to change can be complex.

Recognizing this complexity, attention has been focused in recent years on information system design and implementation as a form of sociotechnical systems intervention. Here we view the organization itself as a sociotechnical system (Trist, 1969). The two fundamental concepts in the sociotechnical perspective are (1) that an organization is the joint interaction of a social system composed of human beings and a technological system composed of tools and techniques, and (2) that each organization or subunit continually interacts with its environment, including the next organizational level where applicable. It seems almost simplistic to state that the implementation of a data-processing system is influenced by and influences both the human and technical aspects of an organization. The process of implementation then can be analyzed as a sociotechnical intervention.

Cummings (1972) has outlined a model of a sociotechnical intervention strategy. The strategy consists of eight sequential stages:

1. defining an experimental system
2. sanctioning an experiment
3. establishing an action group
4. analyzing an experimental system
5. generating hypotheses for redesign
6. testing and evaluating hypotheses for redesign
7. transferring to normal operating system
8. disseminating the results

The stage of the intervention process which is of interest to us (and which corresponds to the situation under investigation) is stage eight, the dissemination of results. In this instance the experimental testing, redesign, and prototype installation has been successfully accomplished. Top management has decided that the change, in this case a computer-based system, has been proven successful, either within the organization or by the vendor of the system. They now desire that it be implemented in multiple organizational sites or units. For reasons already cited, management has determined that the change be propagated throughout the organization without adapting it to the individual units. They want the change (system) to be implemented as is. Cummings elaborates on this stage:

> experience in diffusion of sociotechnical results is limited, two issues appear relevant to the diffusion process. The first is concerned with the content of dissemination. . . . The second involves the process of dissemination. . . . In sum the content and process of disseminating sociotechnical results are important factors in moving the approach to a larger organizational context; as such, they deserve considerable attention and planning.

We are concerned with this final stage of the sociotechnical intervention strategy, the first seven stages having been successfully accomplished. In this last stage, the content of the sociotechnical results to be disseminated has been decided on by top management and we are interested in the process of how these results get moved into a larger organizational context. There has been, as Cummings points out, little or no documentation on how this step is accomplished in the area of computer-based systems.

Thus we are left at a point at which we have (1) a well defined, fixed system which is the intervention we wish to make, and (2) an existing organization in which we want to intervene. We know that using the system will require changes in behavior on the part of the persons within the organization, and possibly change in the structure of the organization. Our job is to determine (1) exactly what these changes should be, and (2) how to bring them about in an acceptable manner.

One body of literature which explicitly deals with eliciting specific changes in personnel behavior is that concerning industrial training. Much of the training literature consists of checklists (e.g., Tracey, 1968 or Swedmark, 1975) or rules of thumb (e.g., Denova, 1971) designed to guide trainers towards "useful" training techniques. A great deal of attention is focused on the learning process itself—the so-called basic principles of human learning (Bass and Vaughan, 1967). In general, the objective pursued is training the individual worker to do a certain job a certain way.

This training literature can prove useful in two ways. The first is in the techniques themselves—at some point in the implementation of a system, specific people must be trained to do specific things. This is particularly true as regards the technical aspects of the system. Once we have decided, for example, who must be trained to operate the hardware, we may profitably turn to proven training methods to help accomplish this (e.g., Bass and Vaughan).

We can also generalize from the training literature a way of approaching the problem which can be of use in thinking through the implementation strategy. This approach, which recurs throughout the training literature (Odiorne, 1970; Singer, 1977; Whitelaw, 1972) basically consists of four steps:

1. Define the organizational objectives toward which the training is directed
2. Define the precise job behavior which the training is to induce, and which is to help meet the organizational objective(s)
3. Analyze this required behavior so as to determine what knowledge, skills and attitudes are required to enable the required behavior

4. Design training activities to provide the subjects with the appropriate knowledge, skills and attitudes

The training literature mostly concerns itself with the fourth step (and with the evaluation of results). However, the general approach outlined above—that is, decide where you're going and then how to get there—provides a basic outline for developing implementation strategy.

In reviewing the literature we have found that the process of managing a standardized system implementation is not addressed directly. It is approached obliquely from several areas, each of which offers some insights into the process. The aim of this research is to synthesize from the literature, and from the researcher's personal experience, a model which does explicitly describe this situation. The goal is, as Keen puts it, "to provide comprehensive explanations in a format that then permits normative recommendations." This research presents a paradigm designed to meet these requirements and attempts to shed light on its validity.

Chapter 3 describes this conceptual scheme, how it might be used, and the research methodology which is employed to evaluate its usefulness.

3

A Conceptual Scheme for Implementation Management and a Methodology for Evaluating It

The Conceptual Scheme

As Ginzberg points out (1976), implementation is a process which accepts certain inputs and produces certain outputs. The output of a successful computer-based system implementation is the use of the system by the organization to perform some task(s). The inputs include the knowledge, skills, and attitudes of the individuals involved, the environment in which they are operating, the task the system is addressing, and the technology itself. Diagrammatically, this is

```
- Individual knowledge,
    skills & attitudes                                          operation of
- Environment              → IMPLEMENTATION →                   the system
- Task(s)                                                       by the users
- Technology (i.e., the
    system itself)
```

In the particular case we are studying, that of mandated implementation of a standardized system, we can refine these inputs and outputs somewhat. On the output side, the fact that top management is ordering use of a standardized system means that "successful" operation can be precisely defined. It consists of a set of activities, events, and outputs which management expects to be forthcoming from the implementing unit. Since the system is already defined, and is not subject to change, these can be specified in advance of implementation.

On the other side, we can divide the inputs into two categories: fixed and variable. In our special case, the system itself and the task(s) it addresses are fixed—management has ordered the implementing unit to use a given system to do a given job. The variable inputs are the knowledge, skills, and attitudes of the individuals involved, and the environment in which they operate. These are the independent variables to be addressed in an attempt to successfully manage the implementation.

The industrial training literature has suggested that determining what knowledge, skills, and attitudes are desired in personnel is best accomplished by first considering the organizational goals involved, and then the specific behaviors needed to achieve those goals. Imposing that structure on the input/output model above, we can synthesize a conceptual scheme which links implementation inputs and outputs.

This scheme, illustrated graphically in Figure 3-1, starts from the idea that the system implementation is being mandated to meet some organizational goal. A technological tool is adopted not as an end in itself, but as a means towards achieving some objective(s). The first step in managing the use of the technological tool should be a careful definition by management of the goals being sought. The model starts with goal definition because of the many cases which have been documented (in what Keen terms the "failure literature") where a lack of such definition was the first step to implementation disaster.

The next step is to explicitly identify exactly what behavior of the organization is implied by, and required to meet, the goals. Only when top management has identified the goals of the implementation can the ranges of organizational behavior be clearly defined. By organizational behavior, in this instance, we are referring to those relevant outputs, activities, and events which are necessary and/or desired to fulfill goal accomplishment. Again, the literature contains examples of implementation failures due at least in part to the fact that the organizations involved never really decided what it was they were trying to accomplish (Lucas, 1975). This level of analysis will result in a listing of the type and sequence of the outputs and activities required to reach the desired goals.

Relevant outputs and activities are nothing more than the aggregate and accumulation of the specific job behaviors of a number of individuals within the organization. When we say, for example, that General Motors makes cars, we are using a shorthand expression to sum up the actions of a large number of people over a period of time. Likewise, when we say that we want a unit to implement a system, we imply specific actions which we want many individuals to perform. Once we have determined what are the desired outputs and activities from the organization as a whole, we can then specify what actions are required from which individuals in the unit or, in other words, what individual job behaviors are needed.

Two sets of factors primarily influence the way in which individuals

Figure 3-1. Implementation Conceptual Scheme

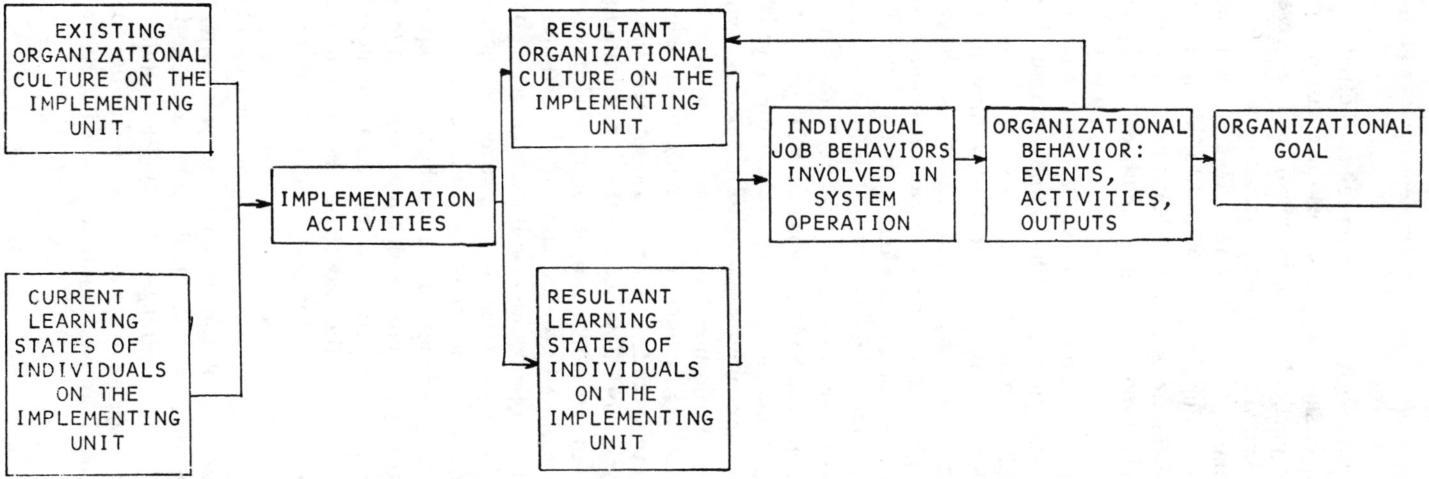

in the organization perform their job-related activities. One of these is the set of knowledge, skills, and attitudes the individual possesses which are relevant to the particular task in question. The presence or absence of these relevant knowledge, skills, and attitudes (KSAs) will be referred to as the individual's "learning state". This is the level of individual preparedness and willingness to perform the desired behavior. The model assumes that there are appropriate learning states for the various individuals which, if achieved, allow the individuals to perform the required task behavior.

As a simple example, consider the task of driving a truck: we can easily identify specific KSAs which a person must have (the presence of which is usually symbolized by possession of a chauffeur's license) in order to properly carry out the task of driving the truck. Likewise, for system implementation, once we have identified the job behaviors needed for successful goal achievement we can (to some extent) identify knowledge, skills, and attitudes individuals should have. Unfortunately, there is seldom a chauffeur's license-type indicator, a simple pass/fail examination, for these kinds of learning states. Both their definition and measurement is a task which remains basically judgmental.

Individual skills and attitudes are not the only influences on job behavior. Another important set of factors, perhaps even more important as an inhibitor of certain behaviors, is what we refer to as the "organizational culture". This includes the formalized systems of authority, analysis, and management as well as more informal systems of communications, work flow, assumptions, and traditions imbedded in the organization. An individual can perfectly well understand how to use a particular system, and even be convinced of its desirability, but still be prevented by the organizational culture from acting on his knowledge and belief (by assumptions such as "we're never the first to install something," for example). The more restrictive aspects (to system implementation) of an organizational culture are those assumptions which managers make, explicitly or implicitly, which have not been tested for their validity and which are not appropriate to the given situation. These can be identified by phrases like, "the way things are done around here", "how we play the game", "our philosophy on doing things", or "people are just that way around here."

When managers hold certain assumptions about their job, organizational goals, aspects of control, or decision-making, then changing their behavior may require first challenging these underlying assumptions (Leonard, 1978). In designing implementation strategy, this organizational setting in which the implementors will be functioning should be assessed for inhibitive assumptions. Some idea of what constitutes an appropriate or "good" organizational culture to facilitate the desired behavior must be formed. Again, this is an area in which the experience and judgment of the person doing the analysis is critical.

It should be noted that the model shows a feedback loop from organizational behavior to organizational culture. As the outputs and activities of an organization change, these changes also influence some of those assumptions (e.g., traditions, rules, customs) and interrelationships which make up its culture. As Leonard points out, the assumptions which predominate in an organization tend to have interconnections, a systemic quality, which often prevent changing just one assumption in an organizational culture. This is one reason why it is often much more feasible to change an organization gradually rather than all at once. Each small change modifies the culture so that the next small change is more readily acceptable. This is encapsulated in the old saw about being able to "walk before you can run."

So far we have been working backwards through the model, determining, in a sense, where we want to go. Before we can decide how to get there (implementation strategy), we need to know our starting point. In the terms of the model, having conceptualized the desired conditions of two sets of influences on individual job behaviors (KSAs and organizational culture), we need to examine the present condition of these two sets. We need to measure the current learning states of key individuals in the implementing units, and we need to identify current critical factors in the organizational culture. To effectively make these measurements, we must have some idea of what it is we are looking for—that is, which knowledge, skills, and attitudes, and which organizational cultural factors are relevant. This step, too, depends on our initial definition of goals and behaviors.

Only after the current status of the learning states and culture and their desired status have been determined should an implementation strategy be developed. Indeed, in the initial process of developing a strategy, we should be continually asking the question, Can we get there from here?

In some cases, we may have to make the decision that successfully implementing the system is too unlikely to warrant an attempt. This decision is, in the broadest sense of the word, an "administrative decision". It involves taking into account a multitude of internal and external forces which might potentially have an impact on any phase of the implementation process. This includes such things as upcoming budget cutbacks, opposing external interest groups, ability of critical people to resist the change, shifting market demands, future financial obligations, and possible personnel transfers. Deciding to abandon the implementation attempt after weighing these factors, while often distasteful, usually results in less disruption than trying the implementation and failing.

Assuming that an administrative decision has been made to proceed with implementation, we now have some guidelines for developing the required implementation activities. We have discovered the "gaps" between the desired and actual learning states, and the implementation activities will be designed to bridge those gaps. At this point we can turn to traditional theories of motivation, training, behavior modification, and so on to help select specific techniques. The process may be an abbreviated one if the system to be installed is simple, the desired behavior straightforward, and the implementation strategists familiar with the current status of the implementing units. To the extent that any of these conditions (system simplicity, directness of behavior, familiarity with unit) are not met, the process will have to be more formal, systematic, and time-consuming.

Research Methodology

The basic hypothesis we want to test is simply whether this way of thinking about the process can be useful in formulating implementation strategy. Does it, in fact, allow us to comprehensively specify all the inputs and outputs in such a way as to suggest courses of action which increase the likelihood of implementation success?

The scheme itself is contentless—that is, it models a general process for which many examples could be given. It suggests a pattern of relationships between inputs and outputs. To test it, therefore, we must observe both the inputs and outputs in situations it purports to describe and attempt to determine whether the actual results are consistent with the expected results. Or, in a more active fashion, we use the scheme to guide us in formulating strategy and evaluate the effects on the results.

The ideal research scenario would involve a large number of identical organizational subunits all being required to implement the same standardized system. In this ideal situation, the researchers would be free to specify the implementation approach (i.e., the treatment) for each unit. We could design strategies for some units which would make success more likely; for others we could design strategies for which failure would be the likely result. We could tie the entire process into an accepted experimental design which would control for all the internal and external sources of invalidity. We could then clinically and statistically evaluate the results and their implications for the model.

Obviously the likelihood of obtaining this ideal research environment is extremely low. The challenge is to work under real world conditions in such a way that one is close enough to the ideal to attempt meaningful research. As mentioned in chapter 1, the U.S. Forest Service offers a set of conditions which do in fact approximate the ideal.

The National Forest System (NFS), the major part of the U.S. Forest Service, consists of 155 national forests scattered mostly throughout the western United States. The forests and their missions are discussed in the next chapter, but it is sufficient for our purposes here to note that they are very similar administrative units. Many of them are quite substantial organizations, with several dozen having annual budgets in excess of five million dollars. In short, the national forests provide a pool of organizational subunits which are comparable, given the proper control factors.

In order to facilitate and standardize parts of the planning and budgeting system in the NFS, top management has mandated that all forests will implement, within the next few years, a computer-based planning system known as ADVENT. This is a standardized package developed by one national forest but currently controlled and maintained centrally. The package will not be altered to fit the desires of any particular forest—all must use it as is. Thus we have precisely the scenario that our research is aimed at exploring: the mandated implementation in multiple organizational subunits of a standardized, computer-based system.

During 1977 and 1978, one NFS region ordered all nineteen of its forests to implement ADVENT immediately. The implementation strategy was simple: management "ordered" it, and technical assistance was made available on a voluntary basis. No attempt was made to assess the needs of individual forests or to tailor the implementation activities to them individually. The results, as documented by McKenney and Gremillion (1978), were mixed.

One year later, another NFS region began implementing ADVENT on its forests. In this case a completely different strategy was adopted. Working with this author regional office staff selected a subset of three forests to implement ADVENT, and designed a tailored implementation strategy for each. The implementation scheme was used to guide the strategy formulation. This is, in effect, a "treatment" group (treatment being the application of individualized strategy), as compared to a "control" group in the previous region.

These two cases give the opportunity for what Campbell and Stanley term the "Recurrent Institutional Cycle Quasi-experimental Design" (Campbell and Stanley, 1973). This design is appropriate to situations in which, on some cyclical basis, new members of an organization are undergoing the same process. It is not a true experiment, since it lacks random assignment of subjects to groups, and simultaneous group formation and measurement. Thus it was necessary to be aware of potential problems with invalidating factors, especially maturation and nonsimilarity. That is, the burden is on the researcher to demonstrate that the members of the two groups are equivalent for the purposes of the experiment, since the design of the experiment does not do this for him automatically.

In reality, this situation is very likely as close as one can come to true experimentation in the area of organizational change. The change itself is well-defined—we know what constitutes implementation success—and therefore, we have a measureable dependent variable. A large number of units are undergoing the same change, and they can be shown to be very similar in all important respects. Different change strategies have been used, with some guided by the model we are trying to validate. The researcher has been given free access to all members of the organizations involved, so that a wide range of possible independent variables can be measured.

Given this setting, we can refine our hypotheses for research into two separate ones:

1. H1: Successful implementation of ADVENT on the forest is closely correlated with identifiable characteristics of the personnel and culture on the forest.
2. H2: Successful implementation of ADVENT on the forest is more likely if the implementation strategy attempts to bring about those characteristics on the implementing unit.

The first hypothesis will be addressed primarily in the case of the first region which employed the undifferentiated strategy. Some forests were successful and some were unsuccessful; we will attempt to discover what characterized each group. In doing so, we will draw largely upon the data collected in the factor study done by Cale (1979). Chapters 5 and 6 describe the observation and data collection in this region, analyze the data, and draw the conclusions concerning the first hypothesis.

Study of this first region will also set up the testing of the second hypothesis in the second region. Once we have determined what characteristics of personnel and culture correlate with success, we are in a position to design implementation strategy to achieve them. This is what is done in the second region.

In the implementations of ADVENT in that region, three steps were taken. First, based on the previous region's experience, it was decided what individual learning states and forest organizational parameters were needed for success. Second, the existing individual and organizational states on the three forests were measured. Finally, a set of implementation activities was designed to help the forests bridge the gaps which were discovered. Chapter 7 describes this process in detail, and chapter 8 describes and analyzes the implementation results.

4

The Research Environment

The organization in which this study has been conducted is the United States Forest Service, an agency of the Department of Agriculture. This chapter provides a brief overview of the mission and organization of the Forest Service as a whole, and of the specific subunits in which the field work was done. Additionally, this chapter describes the program planning process in the National Forest System, and ADVENT, the computer-based program planning system the implementation of which was the vehicle for the research.

The U.S. Forest Service: A Historical Perspective

As a reaction to abusive land use practices of the pioneer era (particularly overcutting of timberlands and overgrazing of range lands), the U.S. Forest Service was created in 1905 to protect certain federal lands. As an agency within the Department of Agriculture, the Forest Service was given the mission of guarding and protecting the Federal Forest Reserves, later to be renamed as National Forests. Between 1905 and 1924, Congress expanded the mission of the Forest Service to include the conducting of forestry research and the promotion of cooperation between federal, state, and private forest interests.

Between this early period and 1940, the predominant concern of the Forest Service was in land preservation. Federal lands were surveyed, mapped, and the resources upon the lands were inventoried. By and large, the major field activities of the forest service aimed at protecting the lands from fire and abusive use. Research efforts centered on minimizing environmental impacts due to land use, and the findings of this research were disseminated to appropriate state as well as private interests.

With the advent of World War II, and with the housing boom of the late 1940s and early 1950s, the role of the Forest Service shifted from one of preservation of natural resources to one of production of forest related commodities, particularly timber. During this period, the major challenge to the Forest Service was to greatly and rapidly increase the production of goods to meet the exploding demands of the War and post-War economy. This emphasis on production lead to increasingly frequent conflicts over resource use. In the 1960s, the heightened public awareness of environmental concerns dramatically increased both the number and intensity of these conflicts.

As a result of these conflicts and the rise in public interest, Congress took a number of legislative actions. The Cooperative Forest Management Act of 1950, the Multiple Use-Sustained Yield Act of 1960, the Wilderness Act of 1964, the National Environmental Policy Act of 1969, the Forest and Rangeland Renewable Resources Planning Act of 1974, and the National Forest Management Act of 1976 were all legislative efforts which, at least in part, were directed at resolving or reducing the impact of such conflicts. In general, these acts modified or established procedures and processes for Forest Service management of lands.

The Forest Service Today

The Forest Service currently is confronted with three major challenges:

1. managing nearly 188 million acres of federal lands in the face of intense and often conflicting demands, within the constraints of complex and often vague legislation
2. continuing to conduct the world's largest program of forestry research
3. increasing and improving the level of cooperation between federal, state, and private forestry interests

The nearly fifty thousand employees of the Forest Service are organized about these three major missions, as shown in Figure 4-1 below. The head of the Forest Service, who reports directly to the Secretary of Agriculture, is the Chief of the Forest Service. The headquarters of the Forest Service, referred to as the Washington Office, is organized as in Figure 4-2. The three major functions of land management, research, and state and private forestry cooperation are each headed by Deputy Chiefs. In addition to these three, there are two other Deputy Chiefs. The Deputy Chief for Administration has responsibility for personnel, accounting, and information services within the Forest Service, while the Deputy Chief for Programs and Legislation is primarily concerned with liaison between the Forest Service, Congress, and other Federal offices.

The responsibility for managing the Forest Service lands falls to the Deputy Chief for the National Forest System. The National Forest System contains all of the National Forests, as well as all individuals directly concerned with the management of those lands. As the field test subjects of this research all function within the National Forest System, the remainder of this chapter will concentrate on that organization.

In describing the management structure of the National Forest System, the Forest Service states that they have

> adopted a line and functional staff combination. The line (i.e. "line of authority") officials within the organization are those that have responsibility for deciding on and activating overall objectives, policies, plans, and programs. The partners in this organizational structure, the staff, advise, recommend, observe, and report. They are responsible for furnishing guidance, assistance, and training.
>
> Successful management of widely separated elements of an organization requires that responsibility be delegated. Within the National Forest System, the delegation concept can be described by the pyramid shown below. Basic delegations are made by the chief to his nine Regional Foresters. Each Regional Forester delegates responsibility to his Forest Supervisors—who, in turn, assign portions of their responsiblity to their District Rangers. (USDA-FS, 1976)

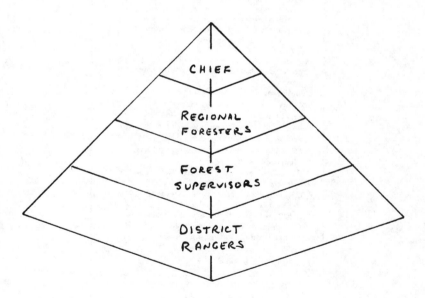

The following paragraphs briefly describe the general responsibilities of each of the four levels of command within the National Forest System.

Figure 4-1. U.S. Department of Agriculture—Forest Service
Activities

NATIONAL FOREST SYSTEM

Protects and manages 187.1 million acres:
- 183.0 million acres National Forests
- 3.8 million acres National Grasslands
- 432,517 acres of Land Utilization Projects, Purchase Units, Research and Experimental Areas, and others.

On these lands are:
- More than 4 million big game animals.
- 217.4 million cu. ft. of standing timber (1970)
- 39 endangered wildlife species.

Fiscal Year 1973 Income:
- $467.6 million from National forests as follows:
  - $446.8 million from timber sales
  - $5.4 million from grazing fees
  - $5.4 million from mineral receipts
  - $8.7 million from recreation admission and user fees

In Fiscal Year 1974:
- $114 million was returned to States

In Fiscal Year 1973:
- 12.4 billion bd. ft. timber harvested (under strict regulation)
- 13.6 billion bd. ft. allowable annual cut
- 1.5 million cattle grazed
- 1.7 million sheep grazed

581 million forest and windbarrier planting stock distributed, under cooperative programs

298,631 acres planted and seeded

52,190 acres of natural regeneration

354,414 acres of stand improvement

106.2 million tree seedlings produced in Federal nurseries

188 million visitor days recreational use (calendar year 1973)

452 miles of road constructed and reconstructed

9,827 miles of road constructed and reconstructed by timber purchasers

106,422 woodland owners assisted, affecting 6.5 million acres; 1.6 million bd. ft. of timber products harvested

13,579 fires promptly controlled

116,705 acres burned

---

9 Regions

---

155 National Forests*

19 National Grasslands*

17 Land Utilization Projects*
12 Nurseries*
682 Ranger Districts*
17 Civilian Conservation Centers

* ADMINISTERED BY 125 SUPERVISORS

MAJOR ACTIVITIES

RESEARCH

Through Science Produces
Knowledge and Technology

for

Managing Resources

  Timber
  Water
  Range
  Wildlife Habitat
  Recreation

Protecting Resources

  Fire
  Insect
  Disease
  Pollution

Utilizing Wood Resources

  Wood Products
  Marketing
  Engineering Systems

Plus

Resource Surveys and
Related Economics

COOPERATION

With

State and Private
Owners
on 574 Million Acres

To

Meet the Needs of an
Expanding Population

Through

Providing Protection
Reforestation
(1.3 Million Acres in 1972)
Increasing Forest Yields
Utilizing Forest Products
Reducing Wood Waste
Conserving Soil
        and Water
Providing Forest
       Recreation
Enhancing Natural Beauty
Increasing Fish and
      Wildlife

---

8 Forest and Range
Experiment Stations

1 Forest Products Laboratory

1 Institute of Tropical Forestry

70 Other Research Locations

---

2 Areas, 7 Regions, and
Institute of Tropical
Forestry

Cooperation with 50
States, Puerto Rico, and
the Virgin Islands

---

325 Research Projects

3,700 Individual Studies

1,112 Scientists

1,300 Publications Annually

Public Agencies,
Community Development
Organizations,
and Forestry Industry

Figure 4-2. Organization of the Forest Service

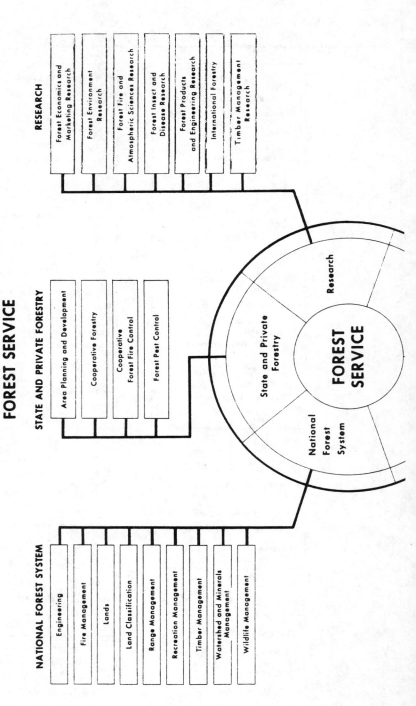

ORGANIZATION CHART

U.S. DEPARTMENT OF AGRICULTURE
FOREST SERVICE

RESEARCH

- Forest Economics and Marketing Research
- Forest Environment Research
- Forest Fire and Atmospheric Sciences Research
- Forest Insect and Disease Research
- Forest Products and Engineering Research
- International Forestry
- Timber Management Research

STATE AND PRIVATE FORESTRY

- Area Planning and Development
- Cooperative Forestry
- Cooperative Forest Fire Control
- Forest Pest Control

NATIONAL FOREST SYSTEM

- Engineering
- Fire Management
- Lands
- Land Classification
- Range Management
- Recreation Management
- Timber Management
- Watershed and Minerals Management
- Wildlife Management

FOREST SERVICE

Research

State and Private Forestry

National Forest System

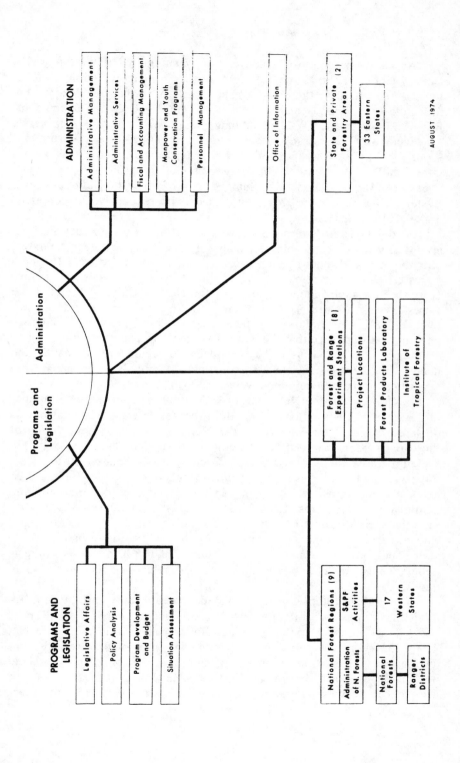

PROGRAMS AND
LEGISLATION

Legislative Affairs

Policy Analysis

Program Development
and Budget

Situation Assessment

Programs and
Legislation

Administration

ADMINISTRATION

Administrative Management

Administrative Services

Fiscal and Accounting Management

Manpower and Youth
Conservation Programs

Personnel Management

Office of Information

State and Private
Forestry Areas (2)

33 Eastern
States

Forest and Range
Experiment Stations (8)

Project Locations

Forest Products Laboratory

Institute of
Tropical Forestry

National Forest Regions (9)

Administration
of N. Forests

S&PF
Activities

National
Forests

17
Western
States

Ranger
Districts

AUGUST 1974

As shown in Figure 4-2 above, the Washington Office staff to the Deputy Chief for the National Forest System are subdivided along functional lines. That is, there are Washington Office staff assigned to the following functional areas of forest management: Timber Management, Range Management, Wildlife Management, Watershed and Minerals Management, Recreation Management, Engineering, Fire Management, Lands, and Lands Classification. The primary function of the Washington Office staff is to recommend nation-wide policy, program and plan objectives to the Deputy Chief. Their major concern is that the National Forest System, as a whole, be managed so as to be responsive to perceived national objectives and needs.

As displayed in Figure 4-3 below, the National Forest System is geographically divided into nine Regions (eight within the lower 48 states, plus the Alaska Region). Each Regional Office is headed by a Regional Forester, who commands an organization typified by Figure 4-4 below. Note that the nine functional areas of the Deputy Chief of the National Forest System are represented, along with State and Private, Administrative, and Planning functions. The primary role of the Regional Office personnel is to ensure that the various National Forests within the region are being managed so as to be responsive to region-wide demands and needs while, at the same time, the region as a whole is being managed in accordance with national objectives.

Each region of the National Forest System is composed of a number of National Forests, about 17 on the average. There are a total of 155 declared National Forests within the National Forest System. Some of these have been administratively combined so that there are only 138 "administrative" National Forests. Each forest is headed by a Forest Supervisor, who controls an organization typified in Figure 4-5. Note that, again, the functional staffs are present, along with various planning and administrative functions. Each National Forest is divided into two types of administrative units: the Supervisor's Office and the Ranger Districts. The Supervisor's office is composed of the Forest Supervisor and his staff. Their primary function is to ensure that the forest as a whole is being managed so as to be responsive to both regional direction and local needs.

The forests themselves are divided geographically into several administrative units called Ranger Districts. Altogether, there are 675 Ranger Districts within the National Forest System, or about four in each forest. The Ranger Districts are the basic units of the National Forest System. The primary responsibility for management and manipulation of the land itself is delegated to the Ranger Districts. Headed by a District Ranger, a typical Ranger District is organized as in Figure 4-6. Again, the functional areas are represented; however, in most cases, one individual will be responsible for more than one functional area. Ranger District personnel are responsible for identifying and executing management activities deemed appropriate and necessary for district lands while, at the same time, contributing their part to overall forest-wide objective. District personnel include professionals, technicians, and often a large force of seasonal laborers.

NFS Region 6

National Forest System Region 6—the Pacific-Northwest region—encompasses the states of Washington and Oregon, in which are nineteen (administrative) National Forests. These forests comprise almost one half of the commercial timber land of the two states, and are critically important both to the local economies and to the nation as a whole as producers of timber. The forests serve as major recreation sources for the area as well.

Region 6 contains several of the largest (in terms of budget and personnel) forests in the system, and is itself the most heavily funded region. In recent years it has been the site of intense conflicts over the uses of the forests, typically between advocates of preserving the forests in their primitive state and those who seek the commodities (e.g., timber) that the forests produce. Other conflicts have centered on the environmental effects of certain forest management practices (for example, disposal of brush by burning and the use of pesticides in forest regeneration).

NFS Region 3

The National Forests of Arizona and New Mexico (National Forest System Region 3) play a special role in that region, as they encompass most of the mountainous (i.e., nondesert) land of the two states. Virtually all of the area's commercial timberland, vital watersheds, valuable grazing lands, unique recreational opportunities, and important wildlife habitats all lie within the National Forest boundaries. The region is comprised of eleven administrative National Forests.

In general, the forests of Region 3 are smaller (in terms of budgets and numbers of personnel) than those in Region 6. No one use dominates the Region 3 forests as timber does in Region 6. However, livestock grazing is an important use on all of the region's forests, and they all experience relatively heavy recreation use, since they are situated on the area's more desirable lands.

Figure 4-3. National Forest System Map

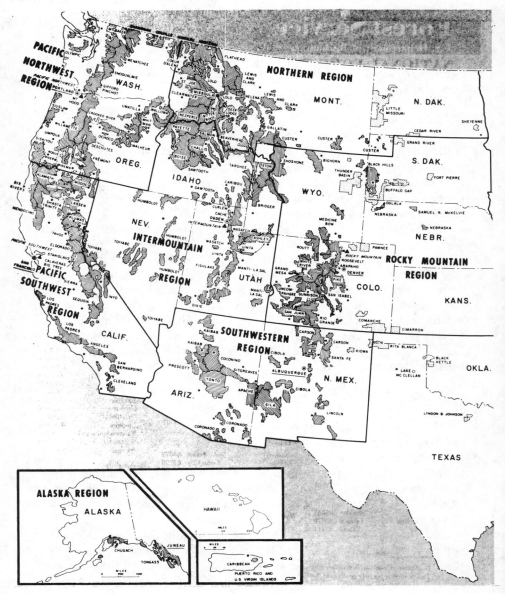

U.S. DEPARTMENT OF AGRICULTURE
FOREST SERVICE
R. MAX PETERSON, CHIEF

NATIONAL FORESTS AND FOREST SERVICE FIELD OFFICES

MILES

	NATIONAL FORESTS
	PURCHASE UNITS
	NATIONAL GRASSLANDS
	LAND UTILIZATION PROJECTS
—	REGIONAL BOUNDARIES
⊙	REGIONAL HEADQUARTERS
•	SUPERVISOR'S HEADQUARTERS
▲	FOREST AND RANGE EXPERIMENT STATIONS
✳	LABORATORY (MADISON, WIS.)
▭	AREA DIRECTOR STATE AND PRIVATE FORESTRY PROGRAMS

March 1980

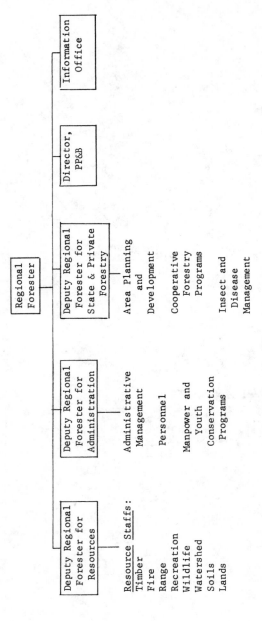

Figure 4-4. Typical Regional Office Organizational Chart

Regional Forester

Deputy Regional Forester for Resources

Deputy Regional Forester for Administration

Deputy Regional Forester for State & Private Forestry

Director, PP&B

Information Office

Resource Staffs:
Timber
Fire
Range
Recreation
Wildlife
Watershed
Soils
Lands

Administrative Management

Personnel

Manpower and Youth Conservation Programs

Area Planning and Development

Cooperative Forestry Programs

Insect and Disease Management

The Program Planning and Budgeting Process

By all measures, the management of the Forest Service presents a massive challenge. Responsible for an area of land nearly the size of Spain and Italy combined, the Forest Service must fulfill its mission with an annual operating budget of about $1.6 billion (Fiscal Year 1978) utilizing the talents of some 20,000 full-time employees spread across the nation. To handle such a task, "the Forest Service has made decentralization its cardinal principle of organization structure, the heart and core of its administrative philosophy" (Kaufman, 1960). However, highly decentralized organizations often present serious coordination and control problems. One of the major tools of the Forest Service for ensuring coordination and control of its diverse units has been the annual budgeting process.

The Forest Service must rely upon annual Congressional appropriations for its operation. Procedurally, the Forest Service develops budget proposals which pass up through the Department of Agriculture and the Office of Management and Budget and are acted upon by Congress. Appropriations, in turn, are divided amongst the various units of the Forest Service on a yearly basis, as received from Congress. As with most federal agencies, the Forest Service is typically working with three budgets at any one time:

1. the current year or action budget, which involves Congressional appropriations for use in the present year
2. next year's budget, which would typically be in some stage of Washington Office, Department, or Congressional review
3. the outyear budget, currently under development in the Forest Service, which will cover activities planned for two years hence

Historically, Forest Service budget plans were developed by the Washington Office functional staff. Each Staff Director, working with his staff counterparts in the Regional Offices, developed a proposed plan for his own resource. The plans were typically based on historical expenditures within a given resource area, with some percentage increase over previous years to account for inflation and modest expansion. Appropriated funds, in turn, flowed through the Staff Directors, through their Regional Office counterparts, and down to the forest level resource staff. Thus, while the line of command in the Forest Service was Chief, Regional Forester, Forest Supervisor, District Ranger, the flow of financial plans and funds went through the resource staffs at each level.

This method of funds planning and distribution was perceived as

Figure 4-5. Two Examples of the Organization of a Typical
            National Forest

Forest Offices - The Forest Supervisor is responsible for the protection,
development, and utilization of all the resources of the National Forest.
There are presently 154 National Forests, but only 129 Forest offices.
This is because one Forest Supervisor's office may administer several
forests. The following charts show two typical organizations of a Forest
Supervisor's Office.

Example No. 1

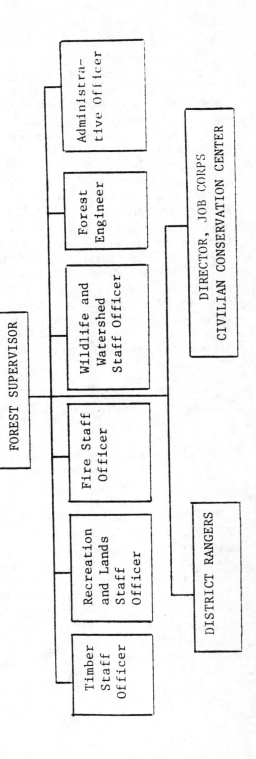

Example No. 2

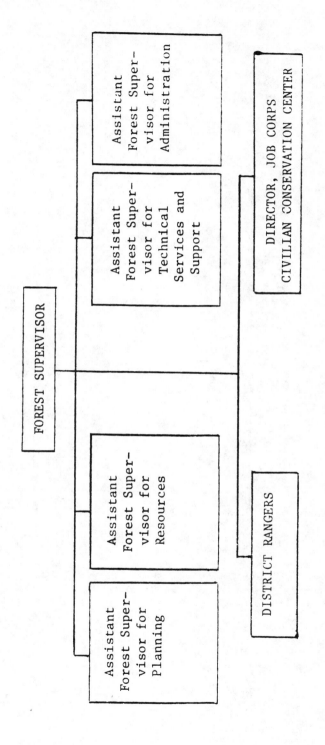

FOREST SUPERVISOR

Assistant Forest Supervisor for Planning

Assistant Forest Supervisor for Resources

Assistant Forest Supervisor for Technical Services and Support

Assistant Forest Supervisor for Administration

DISTRICT RANGERS

DIRECTOR, JOB CORPS CIVILIAN CONSERVATION CENTER

Figure 4-6. Typical Ranger District Organization

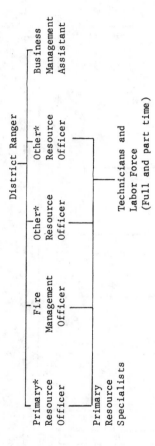

District Ranger

| Primary* Resource Officer | Fire Management Officer | Other* Resource Officer | Other* Resource Officer | Business Management Assistant |

Primary Resource Specialists

Technicians and Labor Force (Full and part time)

*Note: Primary District Staff varies considerably between units, depending on the resource nature of the district. On a Region 6 district, the primary resource officer would be the Timber Management Assistant; on a Region 3 forest, he would be the Range Conservationist. This simply reflects what resource area is most important on that particular district. Typically, two or three other individuals share the other (non-primary) resource areas among themselves, with each covering several areas.

violating certain basic management concepts. Individuals responsible for execution of programs (the line) did not have control over the funding decisions necessary for support of their tasks. Thus, in 1975 the Forest Service significantly modified its budgeting process. A reorganization study under the auspices of the Associate Chief led to the Forest Service adoption of the Program Planning and Budgeting process. Functional staff specialists would no longer have budgetary control; they would function as staff advisors to the line organization, upon which would fall the primary planning and budgeting responsibility. Forest supervisors would develop proposed financial plans for their forests. The regional foresters, in turn, would review and consolidate forest proposals into regional plans, which would then be forwarded to the Chief. Upon receipt of Congressional appropriations, the disbursement of funds would flow back down through the line organization.

Staff input in the planning and distribution decisions would, of course, continue to be vital. However, it was felt that placing ultimate decision authority in the line organization would improve the balance of funding between resources and would increase the line commitment to budgeting goals and objectives. Also, by forcing the proposal development process down to the forest level, it was felt that the plans produced would more accurately reflect the actual needs of the land, allowing the distribution of funds to break with arbitrary historical precedence.

It was felt that for the highly decentralized NFS the most appropriate planning system would be one whose source was as far down in the organization as possible. Ideally, program proposals would be built up on the forests from discretely identified "on the ground" projects. The idea was that building proposals up from the perceived needs of district and forest personnel would be beneficial in two ways. For one thing, this would provide the best available picture of the needs and capabilities of the lands themselves. Additionally, and perhaps of more importance, was the management benefit of this approach—forest managers would feel much more commitment to the programs they were called upon to execute if they could recognize their influence on those programs.

This approach, however, was not without difficulties. One very severe problem was the massive amount of data handling and analysis involved in building forest programs from a number of individual projects. It was found that several hundred projects were required to cover all the proposed activities of all the Ranger Districts on a typical forest. During the fiscal year 1978 program planning effort (winter 1976/77) a number of forests in fact tried this approach to program planning and were so overwhelmed by the mechanics of it that they subsequently abandoned it.

To alleviate this problem, and make the new method of program planning workable, National Forest System Region 5 (California) had developed a computer-based system for handling program planning data. ADVENT, as it was named, was primarily a database management system, although it did also provide a linear programming feature for optimizing project selection. Each project within ADVENT is composed of a time series of inputs (usually man-hours and dollars required to complete the project) and outputs (such as the timber the project will produce). The user can aggregate the projects into programs either by manually selecting groups of projects or by using the LP feature with appropriate objective function and constraints. The major benefit of ADVENT had proved to be reformatting, aggregating and cross-referencing the system performed automatically to provide management with the measurements they needed to analyze the program proposals.

By 1977 it was apparent to NFS management that such a computer-based program planning system should be used on all the National Forests. The Chief's Office ordered a two-part implementation: forests would begin implementing a current version of ADVENT, while the USFS management science group studied the need for further improvements. All forests would be required to have the system installed by the fiscal year 1983 program planning effort. Regional offices were to be responsible for implementation on their forests, and a coordinating group was established in the Washington Office.

The Washington Office coordinating group was headed by personnel from the Program Development and Budget office, with which the Harvard Business School Cooperative Study Team had been working for the previous year. Since the team had done an analysis of NFS program planning the year before, it was invited to observe and help with the ADVENT implementation. It was through this invitation that this author was able to conduct the field work involved in the research presented in this study.

NFS Regions 6 and 3 adopted quite different approaches towards implementing ADVENT on their forests. Chapter 5 describes the Region 6 implementation activities and the clinical observation made of those activities and their results, while chapter 6 analyzes those observations and presents the implementation concepts suggested by them. Chapter 7 then describes the development and execution of the Region 3 implementation strategy in light of that conceptual scheme. Finally, chapter 8 describes and analyzes the results of the Region 3 experiences.

5

Region 6 ADVENT Implementations

Background

NFS Region 6 (Pacific Northwest) adopted the new Program Planning and Budget process in 1975. The first program planning cycle took place during the fall, winter, and spring of 1975/76, and was aimed at producing program proposals for the fiscal year 1978. The newly formed regional Program Planning and Budget (PPB) office developed the Region 6 procedures and coordinated their execution. Each of the region's nineteen forests developed individual program plans, which the regional PPB staff consolidated into regional plans.

In line with the Chief's directives in instituting the PPB system, the Region 6 forests were encouraged to heavily involve ranger district personnel in generating their program proposals. The ideal forest process was seen to be one in which ranger district personnel generated a large number of feasible site-specific projects, which were then selected and aggregated to form the forest program plans. All of the forests pursued this approach to a greater or lesser extent. Problems, however, became immediately apparent.

Although some of the difficulties which arose stemmed from inexperience on the part of the personnel involved, most arose from a characteristic unavoidable in the site-specific project approach—the massive amount of data handling involved. Overwhelmed by the time-consuming efforts required to collect, edit, analyze, and reformat the data, many forests and districts were forced to devote inordinate amounts of manpower to the process or miss deadlines. Some forests even abandoned the project-based approach and merely extrapolated historical trend data to develop their program plans. Many forest personnel were left with very negative feelings about the process, feelings which were still evident in the summer of 1977 when they were interviewed concerning the program planning process. (McKenney et. al., 1978)

The planning cycle for fiscal year 1979 (fall/winter/spring, 1976/77) saw most Region 6 forests pull back from the project-based program planning approach. Typical practice this time around was to have the Forest Supervisor's office staff prepare programs in their particular functional areas using historical cost and output figures. This, of course, was a step backwards from the desired program planning procedure.

In order to reverse this trend, the regional office PPB staff realized that it would be necessary to solve the data handling problem. As a result, they decided to have the forests implement ADVENT, the program planning DBMS, as soon as possible. It was decided that all forests would be required to use ADVENT, to some extent, in preparing the fiscal year 1980 program proposals. The forests were given some leeway, however, as to the exact approach they employed.

The regional office staff presented the forests with three alternative approaches to using ADVENT:

1. They could have the ranger districts prepare site-specific projects describing feasible work activities on the forest. These would be fed into ADVENT, which would then be used to manipulate and analyze them, and, finally, aggregate them into forest program plans. The proposals would be electronically transmitted to the regional office as an ADVENT database. This approach most closely approximated the "ideal" or "full" ADVENT implementation.

2. They could develop "pseudo-projects" which were not site-specific, and which typically would represent the total alternative program for one resource system on one ranger district. For example, the entire timber program on a district would make up one such pseudo-project (whereas with the site-specific approach, that district's timber program would be represented by dozens of separate projects—timber sales, reforestation projects, etc.). This approach reduced the number of projects to be generated by a factor of six to eight. These pseudo-projects were entered into ADVENT, and the same aggregation and transmittal performed as in the previous alternative.

3. The lowest level of ADVENT implementation merely required that the forests submit their program proposals to the regional office in ADVENT data format. The forest was free to actually develop the proposals by whatever method they chose. They would then input the programs themselves as pseudo-projects into the ADVENT database. The total forest program for a resource system would make up one such pseudo-project.

   The regional office PPB staff's long-term goal was to have all forests "fully" implement ADVENT (i.e., alternative 1) within the next three years. They did not have the resources, however, either in manpower or management support, to require full implementation on all forests in the first year. The strategy adopted was one of successive approximations to the final goal. All forests were required to perform at least the baseline implementation during the first year. Forests which were interested could make more extensive use of the analytical and data display features of the package. Forests which were not interested in using the system could prepare their program plans however they wanted, and then merely transcribe them into the proper format. Even these forests, however, might learn something about ADVENT and the site-specific approach to program planning. If nothing else, the supervisor's office staff was introduced to some new concepts and technology. Given this incremental learning, it was felt that it should be easier to induce the forest to make somewhat more extensive use of the system in subsequent planning cycles.

   The regional office's short-range implementation strategy for this year was quite simple because of this long-range strategy. The initiation was purely by decree—a letter from the Regional Forester instructed all forests to implement the system with the options described above. Forests were further informed that technical training and assistance would be available, but purely on a voluntary basis. No attempt was made to evaluate any forest's states of readiness and to tailor the training accordingly.

   With a passive and undifferentiated implementation strategy such as this one, we can hypothesize that the implementation results would be strongly correlated with the initial states of readiness on the forests. Indeed, these initial states of readiness form the only source of variability. The implementation activities designed by the regional office by design were applied to all forests evenly. The task in examining this hypothesis, then, requires observation and quantification of both the states of readiness and degrees of success of the forests. The following section describes how this was accomplished.

Data Collection in Region 6

The ADVENT implementation in Region 6 was under study by Cale (1979), whose goal was to demonstrate the relationship between a number of organizational and individual factors and implementation success. Thus the measurements needed to test the first hypothesis were being made to support this factor study. The present author, in fact, was part of the team making the observations.

   As Cale points out, the Region 6 implementations made an ideal testbed for a number of reasons. The fact that there were nineteen implementing units provides a fairly large sample size, especially for this type of research. Since all the forests are part of the same organization and have very similar missions, they come close to being, for experimental purposes, identical units. However, the variability of management style, information system sophistication, and experience across the forests assured a rich mixture of different states of readiness. Finally, the time frame for implementation was finite and well-defined, therefore providing a natural framework for observation and evaluation.

The approach taken to data collection and analysis was similar to that taken by Zalesnik, Christiansen, and Roethlisberger in their classic study of worker productivity (1958). This involved extensive clinical observation of the subject organizations before, during, and after the implementation period. Both subjective and objective measurements were obtained through a variety of means (to be discussed below). These data were then preprocessed into indices of organizational and individual factors which might be related to implementation success. Finally, quantitative data analysis techniques were used to evaluate the relationships among these indices and their correlations with implementation success.

The data collection effort is described below. The preprocessing, data analysis, and conclusions are discussed in chapter 6.

Data Collection—Implementing Units

States of readiness data (i.e., the independent variable readings) were collected from forest personnel both prior to and after attempted ADVENT implementations. As Cale points out, however, these measurements are primarily of the forests' states of readiness prior to the (minimal) implementation strategy execution by the regional office. Factors which might have changed during the implementation—management attitudes, for example—were measured prior to implementation. Some measurements of objective data, like the programming method used on the forest for fiscal year 1979, were not actually made until after the implementations. Preimplementation measurements were made primarily at the three day regional office training sessions conducted in October/November 1977. Postimplementation measurements were made during visits to each of the forests in April, 1978. Data was collected using both questionnaires and tightly guided interviews. (See Appendix A for sample questionnaires and interview guidelines.) Information from personnel not available during these periods was collected by telephone and/or mail.

At least the Forest Supervisor and the program planning leader were interviewed on each forest. Any other person who played an important role in the program planning effort—such as the computer specialist, in some cases—was also interviewed. The program planning leader was that member of the forest staff who was primarily responsible for producing the program plans. The exact organizational location of this individual varied from forest to forest.

Data Collection—Regional Office

One major specification in the research design concerned the definition of success. The type of implementation under study was (1) of a standardized, predefined system, which would not be tailored, and (2) ordered by an organizational superior. Success, therefore, is defined from the point of view of that organizational superior, and is the degree to which the implementing unit's actual use of the system is congruent with the superior's intended use. In the Region 6 ADVENT implementations, therefore, it was the responsibility of the regional office PPB staff to evaluate the success of the forests.

This was done along two dimensions. The first concerned itself with the approach to ADVENT use which the forest took. The three alternatives—site-specific, district-specific, and forest-wide—are described above. In addition, the regional office staff determined that two other "mixed" approaches should be distinguished. One of these was basically a district-specific programming approach, but with site-specific projects used in some resource systems. The other was basically a forest-wide approach, but with district-specificity in some resource areas. A scale from one to five was used, with five corresponding to the "full" or "ideal" implementation, and one representing the approach furthest from the ideal. Each forest was assigned to one of these categories. This was a fairly objective measurement, since the forest databases could be examined and their level of detail determined both by the regional office staff and by the researchers.

The second measurement was a more subjective one made by the regional office staff. On a one to five scale, the staff rated the forest on how "good a job" they had done, given the approach they adopted. This judgment was based, in large part, on the extent to which the forest made use of the features of the ADVENT system in preparing their plans. The extent to which ADVENT-assisted analysis had enabled the forest management to make decisions about their program proposals was considered a crucial issue. A forest which merely put its data into the ADVENT format, but made no other use of the tool, was rated at one. Forests which made use of the analytical and data management capabilities of the system to improve the quality of their program plans were rated more highly according to their degree of use.

Figure 5-1 shows a distribution of the forests according to the approach taken and the regional office evaluation of their success. A forest rated 5,5 was a total success; a 1,1 forest was a miserable failure. As Figure 5-1 illustrates, there was considerable variability among the forests as to implementation outcome, an encouraging characteristic for dependent variables. The task now is to identify predictor variables and examine their relationships to these outcome measurements. That task is taken up in chapter 6.

Figure 5-1.   Distribution of the Nineteen Region 6 Forests
              According to the ADVENT Approach Selected and
              the Degree of Success Achieved.

		1	2	3	4	5
	5	0	0	1	2	1
Approach						
Attempted	**4**	0	0	1	1	2
by the						
Forest	**3**	0	0	1	1	1
	2	0	0	1	1	1
	1	1	4	0	0	1

Degree of Success Achieved by the Forest, Given the Approach Selected

6

Analysis of the Region 6 Implementations

In his factor study of implementation strategy, Cale hypothesized five factors which would be correlated with implementation success. These were:

1. The relative advantage which the potential users perceived of the new system over their present procedures
2. The complexity of the system relative to their technical skills
3. The compatibility between the procedures required by the system and existing practice in the organization
4. The potential user's perception of how much weight his superior would place on successful implementation
5. The potential user's opportunity to try the system before committing to it irrevocably

These hypothesized factors guided the data collection effort in Region 6. The design of questionnaires and interviews was motivated by the need to eventually be able to rate the implementing units along these five dimensions. As described earlier, a large number of clinical observations were made at several points in time. A two-step process was followed to reduce these observations to measurements along the desired dimensions.

First, the raw data was collected. This was then preprocessed into twenty-five "indices", or variables, each of which rated the forest along some dimension related to one or more of the factors. Finally, statistical analyses were made on these indices to aggregate them into factors such as those hypothesized which could be correlated with the units' implementation success.

It was necessary to collect such a large amount of data because of the difficulty in precisely rendering the hypothesized factors operational. Obviously each of the factors summarized a number of skills and attitudes of a number of individuals on the forests. Take, for example, the second factor, relative complexity. This is a measure of how capable the forest is of handling the technical demands of the system. Since "full" use of the ADVENT system involves all levels of forest management, the skills of a number of people influence this measurement. Furthermore, both an individual's skills in program planning and computer-based processes in general and his skill in the ADVENT system itself apply. Thus, a number of indices were used to try and cover the various facets of the factors. The twenty-five indices which were developed are listed below. All of these, except where noted, employ a one to five scale with lower values representing conditions thought to be less favorable to successful implementation. The following abbreviations are used: FS (Forest Supervisor, PPL (Program Planning Leader), RF (Regional Forester).

1. *FS Opinion on Planning/Budget Link*: To what extent does the forest supervisor believe that the program plans he submits determine the budget allocation he receives? (1 = not at all; 5 = closely correlated)

2. *PPL Opinion on Planning/Budget Link*: To what extent does the program planning leader feel that the program plans submitted determine the budget allocation? (1 = not at all; 5 = closely correlated)

3. *FS Opinion on Site-Specific Approach*: To what extent does the forest supervisor believe that the use of site-specific projects in program planning improves the accuracy of the plans? (1 = not at all; 5 = great improvement)

4. *PPL Opinion on Site-Specific Approach*: To what extent does the program planning leader believe that the use of site-specific projects in program planning improves the accuracy of the plans? (1 = not at all; 5 = great improvement)

5. *FS on Program Planning as a Management Tool*: Does the forest supervisor feel that the program planning process is of benefit to forest management, other than merely as a means to request funding? (1 = no usefulness; 5 = very useful)

6. *PPL on Program Planning as a Management Tool*: To what extent does the program planning leader feel that program planning is of use in managing the forest, other than as a means of requesting funding? (1 = no use; 5 = very useful)

7. *FS Opinion of Manpower Impact*: What is the forest supervisor's perception of the manpower required to develop program plans using ADVENT as compared to that required by the method the forest used last year? (1 = ADVENT much more time-consuming; 5 = ADVENT much less time-consuming)

8. *PPL Opinion of Manpower Impact*: What is the program plan-

ning leader's perception of the manpower required to develop program plans using ADVENT as compared with that required by the method used last year? (1 = ADVENT much more time-consuming; 5 = ADVENT much less time-consuming)

9. *FS Overall Opinion of ADVENT*: What is the forest supervisor's overall expressed opinion of the ADVENT system? (1 = very negative; 5 = very positive)

10. *PPL Overall Opinion of ADVENT*: What is the program planning leader's overall expressed opinion of ADVENT? (1 = very negative; 5 = very positive)

11. *RO Evaluation of Forest Computer Skill*: How does the regional office PPB staff rate the competance of the forest's computer specialist? (1 = no computer competence on forest; 5 = very competent)

12. *FS Exposure to Computers*: To what extent has the forest supervisor been exposed in the past to the use of computer-based systems? (1 = not at all; 5 = considerable exposure)

13. *PPL Exposure to Computers*: To what extent has the program planning leader been exposed in the past to computer-based systems? (1 = not at all; 5 = considerable exposure)

14. *FS Familiarity with ADVENT*: To what extent is the forest supervisor familiar with the features and capabilities of ADVENT? (1 = not at all; 5 = very knowledgeable)

15. *PPL Familiarity with ADVENT*: To what extent is the program planning leader familiar with the features and capabilities of ADVENT? (1 = not at all; 5 = very knowledgeable)

16. *FS Understanding of Linear Programming*: To what extent does the forest supervisor understand linear programming? (1 = not at all; 5 = very well)

17. *PPL Understanding of Linear Programming*: To what extent does the program planning leader understand linear programming? (1 = not at all; 5 = very well)

18. *Previous Management Role in Program Planning*: In developing the fiscal year 1979 program proposals, how widespread was forest management participation? (1 = minimal participation; 5 = full participation)

19. *Previous Data Specificity in Program Planning*: In developing the fiscal year 1979 program plans, what degree of data specificity did the forest use? (1 = forest wide aggregations; 5 = site-specific projects)

20. *Previous PPL Role in Program Planning*: In developing the fiscal year 1979 program plans, how compatible was the role played

by the program planning leader with that he would play in the "full" ADVENT implementation? (1 = not at all alike; 5 = basically the same role)

21. *Previous Data Handling Method*: In developing the fiscal year 1979 program plans, to what extent did the program planning leader manipulate ADVENT-like planning data? (1 = no data manipulation; 5 = performed ADVENT-like data manipulation of site-specific project data)

22. *Previous Management Experience with ADVENT*: To what extent has management on the forest had previous experience with ADVENT? (1 = no one; 3 = some individuals; 5 = widespread experience)

23. *PPL Previous Experience with ADVENT*: To what extent has the program planning leader had experience with ADVENT? (1 = not at all; 3 = indirect experience; 5 = has used the system himself)

24. *FS Demonstration of Commitment to Process*: What is the program planning leader's perception of the forest supervisor's interest in the *process* of generating program plans? (1 = doesn't care about process; 5 = very interested in process)

25. *FS Demonstration of Commitment to ADVENT*: What is the program planning leader's perception of how important it is to the forest supervisor that ADVENT be used in developing the program plans? (1 = not important at all; 5 = very important)

26. *RF Demonstration of Commitment to ADVENT*: What is the forest supervisor's perception of how important it is to the Regional Forester that ADVENT be used in developing the program plans? (NOTE: on all forests, the supervisors' perception was that the regional forester did not at all care whether they used ADVENT or not. Since this variable would, therefore, have a constant value of 1, it is dropped from the analysis.)

Appendix B shows the values of each of these variables (numbered as above) for each of the nineteen forests. As an example of how these indices were formulated, consider number 16—the forest supervisor's understanding of linear programming. The actual question asked in the interview was, "If one of your fellow supervisors asked you what linear programming is, and how it is useful in program planning, how would you respond?" The interviewer pressed the supervisor, if necessary, to state exactly what he would say in response to such a question and this was recorded. The interviewer also played the role of the peer asking the question and requested the supervisor to elaborate on any parts of his answer which were unclear. From this the researchers were able to make an evaluation of the level of understanding which the supervisor had for this particular aspect of ADVENT. The other indices were constructed similarly.

Even to the casual observer it is apparent that these indices overlap quite a bit. Indices 1, 3, 5, 7, and 9, for example, all of which are concerned with the forest supervisor's feelings about program planning and ADVENT, are likely to move closely together for each supervisor. In more technical terms, there is a great deal of intercorrelation among the independent variables.

On the other hand, each index does in fact make some at least slightly different measurement. Take indices 1 and 5 for example—both attempt to measure the supervisor's opinion of the usefulness of program planning. Each, however, is concerned with a different reason why the supervisor might consider it a useful process; and these reasons, while usually related, could very possibly be independent. It is therefore necessary to take a large number of overlapping measurements to try to ensure that all pertinent sources of variability are captured.

Our primary interest is not in the twenty-five intercorrelated indices, but rather in the more basic factors which underly them. To explore these, an appropriate data analysis technique is factor analysis. In factor analysis, "an attempt is made to 'explain' the observed correlations by assuming that there exist some unobservable 'factors' each of which affects several or all of the variables" (Schlaifer, 1978). It is possible to find an infinite number of sets of factors which explain the correlations among the variables. While most of these make no intuitive "sense", interesting interpretations can often be found when the factor patterns have a very loosely defined property called "simplicity". Simplicity, or interpretability, of a factor pattern is judged by the extent to which each variable seems to be "mostly explained" by one factor, and "very little explained" by the others. Additionally, simplicity implies that each factor contributes heavily to the explanation of a different subset of variables. This means that we want to have one group of variables which basically represents one factor, another separate group of variables which basically represents another factor, and so on.

Extracting factors from the twenty-five indices may be thought of as defining the states of readiness of the forests which these indices, imprecisely and with much overlap, measure. The first task in the data analysis, then, is to determine if an intuitively acceptable factor pattern can be developed and interpreted. A number of factor analyses were run on the forest data, with different numbers of factors and other parameter specifications. Table 6-1 shows the factor pattern for a four factor analysis, after a varimax rotation. The variable numbers listed in the leftmost column of this table correspond to the numbers of the indices listed above. The numbers in the row for each variable are the loadings of that variable on the factors.

The variables which load most heavily on factor 1 (i.e., 18, 19, 20, 21) are those which measure the compatibility between ADVENT-assisted program planning and the method previously used by the forest. Variables 4, 10, and 13, which also load heavily on factor 1, measure the program planning leader's opinion of and experience with the ADVENT-assisted process. This factor can be interpreted as representing the familiarity of the forest management with the ADVENT process—is it like what they've been doing before, and does the process leader feel comfortable with it?

The variables which load heavily on factor 2 (1, 3, 5, 7, 9, 14, 16, 22, 24, 25) almost all concern the forest supervisor. Some of these measure the attitude of the supervisor towards program planning itself (1, 3, 5); some measure his attitude towards the ADVENT system (7, 9); and some measure his understanding of how the tool works (14, 16). Some of the variables measure the program planning leader's perception of the forest supervisor's attitudes towards the process (24, 25). Factor 2 can be interpreted as the forest supervisor's commitment to and demonstration of commitment to the ADVENT-assisted program planning process.

Factor 3 shows heavy loadings from the variables which measure the program planning leader's understanding of the ADVENT computer-based system itself. Variables 15 and 17 attempt to measure this directly. Variable 8 does so indirectly—the comparison the program planner makes between ADVENT and another programming method reflects, among other things, his understanding of ADVENT. Factor 3 may be interpreted as the forest planning staff's understanding of the tool.

Variables 11, 12, and 13 load most heavily on factor 4. All of these measure the degree to which the forest management and staff are competant with computer-based systems. Variable 11 is the regional staff's evaluation of the forest's computer capability. Variables 12 and 13 are the researchers' evaluations of the competance of the forest supervisor and program planner, respectively. Factor 4 may be interpreted as the forest's computer familiarity.

Thus we have four intuitively acceptable factors or states of readiness identified:

1. The familiarity of the forest management and staff with the site-specific project-based ADVENT-assisted program planning process

Table 6-1. Factor Loadings for a Four-Factor, Varimax Rotated Factor Analysis of the Twenty-Five Indices. Variables have been re-ordered to highlight the factor pattern. (Note: FS = Forest Supervisor; PPL = Program Planning Leader.)

Variables	Loadings on Factors			
	1 Process Familiarity	2 Supervisor Commitment	3 PPL Competance	4 Computer Skills
4-PPL Opinion on Site-Specific Approach	0.55	0.17	0.39	0.07
10-PPL Overall Opinion of ADVENT	0.67	0.36	0.41	0.08
18-Previous Management Role in Program Planning	0.92	0.24	0.17	0.01
19-Previous Data Specificity in Program Plng	0.91	0.28	0.06	0.11
20-Previous PPL Role in Program Planning	0.94	0.18	0.18	0.10
21-Previous PPL Role in Data Handling	0.93	0.14	0.13	0.06
23-PPL Previous ADVENT Experience	0.43	0.23	0.24	0.04
1-FS Opinion on Planning/Budget Link	-0.11	0.53	-0.02	0.03
3-FS Opinion on Site-Specific Approach	0.57	0.62	-0.13	0.10
5-FS on Prog Plng as a Management Tool	0.47	0.78	-0.02	0.11
6-PPL on Prog Plng as a Management Tool	0.45	0.54	0.18	0.02
7-FS Opinion on Manpower Impact	0.40	0.47	0.29	0.32
9-FS Overall Opinion of ADVENT	0.45	0.75	0.18	0.04
14-FS Familiarity with ADVENT	0.52	0.60	0.26	0.30
16-FS Familiarity with Linear Programming	0.40	0.59	0.31	0.31
22-Previous Mgmt Experience with ADVENT	0.36	0.45	-0.08	0.21
24-FS demonstration of Commitment to Process	0.39	0.74	0.26	0.23
25-FS Demonstration of commitment to ADVENT	0.17	0.69	0.40	0.10
8-PPL Opinion on Manpower Impact	0.13	0.30	0.50	0.41
15-PPL Familiarity with ADVENT	0.18	0.21	0.81	0.32
17-PPL Familiarity with LP	0.28	-0.04	0.90	0.09
2-PPL Opinion on Planning/Budget Link	-0.16	0.21	-0.05	0.31
11-RO Evaluation of Forest Comp. Skill	0.06	-0.04	-0.01	0.64
12-FS Exposure to Computers	-0.11	0.05	0.10	0.86
13-PPL Exposure to Computers	0.23	-0.15	0.31	0.62

2. The commitment of the forest supervisor to the process and his demonstration to his subordinates of that commitment
3. The familiarity of the program planner(s) with the ADVENT system itself
4. The general familiarity of forest management with computer-based systems

The next step is to determine what relationships exist between these measures and the degree of success each forest achieved with its implementation.

The relationships are illustrated most simply by looking at the correlations between the scores for the forests on each of the factors and their degree of success. Figure 6-1 shows these correlations. Obviously, there are strong correlations between factor 1, familiarity with the process, and both the approach selected and degree of success. This implies that the more accustomed forest management is to the site-specific, ADVENT-assisted approach, the more likely they are to (1) adopt that approach, and (2) be successful in their efforts. The implication for strategy formulation is that this familiarity should be supplied, probably through training, where it doesn't already exist.

Factor 2, the supervisor's commitment and demonstration of commitment, correlates with the degree of success enjoyed, but correlates even more strongly with the approach taken. The conclusion here is that

Figure 6-1. Correlations between General Factors and Measures of Success for Region 6 Forests Implementing ADVENT.

| | Measures of Success | |
| | Approach Attempted | Degree of Success Achieved |
General Factors		
1. Familiarity of Forest Staff with the site-specific project approach	.5798	.6080
2. Forest Supervisor's demonstration of commitment	.7086	.4165
3. Program Planning leader's familiarity with ADVENT	.2902	.3302
4. General familiarity of forest management with computer-based systems	−.0796	.2326

"selling" the forest supervisor on the process is necessary in order to move the forest in the desired direction. The implication for strategy formulation here is clear—the first step must be to ensure the supervisor's commitment. Furthermore, this is one of the most important steps in the process of achieving implementation and deserves considerable attention. This factor was not addressed at all in the Region 6 implementation strategy.

Factor 3, the forest planning staff's familiarity with ADVENT, is positively correlated with both the approach attempted and the degree of success, although the correlations are not as strong as with factors 1 and 2. Clearly, it helps to have a process leader who is competent with the system. This factor, however, can be dominated by the first two, if the supervisor is sold on the system and the forest staff is generally familiar with the site-specific project approach. In such a case, the program planning leader is under considerable pressure to learn how to use the system if he doesn't know how already. He could do this by reading the documentation and/or attending the regional office's training sessions.

The familiarity of forest management with computer technology, factor 4, does not correlate with approach selected, and only weakly correlates with the degree of success achieved. To some extent this may be explained as being due to the domination of the other factors—if the supervisor is committed and the staff competent, then the forest will attempt a more advanced approach, believing that they will be able to acquire the necessary computer skills. This is also the one area in which Region 6 may have had something of an implementation strategy. "Canned", or predefined jobstreams were provided to allow the forests to run the ADVENT programs, and, in fact, some of the computer work was done from the regional office. Thus the forests were, to some extent, insulated from the technical details of running the computer system if they wanted to be so insulated. Even so, a weak correlation remains, implying that forests with a greater computer capability are more likely to be successful in using this computer-based system.

Table 6-2 shows the correlations between the two measures of success and each of the twenty-five indices used. For the most part this merely shows the same things as the correlations between the factors and success. A few interesting insights can be gained from this more detailed examination, however.

One thing which is immediately apparent is that the variables most strongly correlated with both approach attempted (3, 5, 7, 9, 24) and with the degree of success (14, 16) involve the forest supervisor. Clearly, if there is to be a successful implementation, the supervisor must (1) understand what ADVENT-assisted program planning involves,

56   *Analysis of the Region 6 Implementations*

Table 6-2.   Correlations Between the Twenty-Five Indices and the
Measures of Success for the Region 6 Forests.
Results have been sorted in decreasing order of magnitude by
correlation between the variable and the approach attempted.

| | Correlation with: | |
Variable	Approach Attempted	Degree of Success
3-FS Opinion on Site-Specific Approach	0.79	0.50
9-FS Overall Opinion of ADVENT	0.78	0.67
5-FS on Prog Plng as Management Tool	0.75	0.53
7-FS Opinion on Manpower Impact	0.73	0.41
24-FS Demo of Commitment to Process	0.71	0.51
18-Previous Mgmt Role in Prog Plng	0.66	0.64
25-FS Demo of Commitment to ADVENT	0.63	0.37
4-PPL Opinion on Site-Specific App	0.63	0.34
20-Previous PPL Role in Prog Plng	0.62	0.63
19-Previous Data Specificity in Prog Plng	0.60	0.63
14-FS Familiarity with ADVENT	0.60	0.84
8-PPL Opinion on Manpower Impact	0.57	0.07
6-PPL on Prog Plng as Management Tool	0.55	0.47
10-PPL Overall Opinion of ADVENT	0.53	0.43
22-Previous Mgmt Experience with ADVENT	0.52	0.16
21-Previous PPL Role in Prog Planning	0.50	0.59
15-PPL Familiarity with ADVENT	0.50	0.48
23-PPL Previous ADVENT Experience	0.48	0.31
1-FS Opinion on Planning/Budget Link	0.33	−0.02
17-PPL Familiarity with LP	0.27	0.51
11-RO Evaluation of Forest Comp. Skill	0.14	0.25
2-PPL Opinion on Plng/Budget Link	−0.06	−0.02
12-FS Exposure to Computers	0.05	0.11
13-PPL Exposure to Computers	0.05	0.13

Abbreviations used above: FS—Forest Supervisor
PPL—Program Planning Leader
LP—Linear Programming
RO—Regional Office

(2) believe that there is some benefit in adopting the process, and (3) make his belief known to his subordinates.

Table 6-2 again shows the lack of significant correlation between the forests' computer skills (variables 11, 12, 13) and either measure of success. Although this seems rather counterintuitive, it may be rationalized in a number of ways. For one thing, all the forests in Region 6 had at least a basic level of computer expertise, enough to execute most of the simpler ADVENT jobstreams. The regional office took some responsibility off the forest computer specialist by providing prewritten jobstreams. Finally, in a few cases, the forest computer specialist was called into the regional office to work with staff personnel, or the regional staff simply ran the ADVENT jobs for the forests themselves. Because of all of this, forests were able to get around any shortcomings in computer skills they may have had.

Conclusions

Figure 6-2 illustrates graphically Region 6's implementation strategy in the format of the conceptual scheme. Clearly, the strategy was oriented strictly towards the technical aspects of the system. The regional office staff had some important constraints within which they had to operate when designing and executing the implementation strategy. The top line officer, the Regional Forester, was very new on the job and was preoccupied with public policy controversies on herbicide use and roadless area studies during most of the time the regional office was preparing the fiscal year 1980 programming. As a result, the direct line management involvement in the process which the PPB staff would have desired was not available. In practice, the ADVENT implementation would have to be something worked out between the regional PPB staff and the program planning leader on the forest. On most forests this was the budget officer or equivalent, a person two levels below the forest supervisor. This imposed severe limits on the extent to which the regional staff could direct the forest process. Therefore the only behavior actually required of the organizations was the "baseline" implementation—that is, the forests had to submit their data in ADVENT format, regardless of how that data was originally generated.

To achieve this level of implementation, a relatively simple strategy was thought appropriate. For one thing, the job behavior of only a small subset of forest personnel was critical: that of the PPB staff and computer persons who must make sure the data is put into the proper format. The forest supervisor, resource staff personnel, and district rangers could continue to program in whatever their usual way has been. All that was

Figure 6-2. NFS Region 6 ADVENT Implementation Strategy, Fiscal Year 1980 Program Planning Cycle

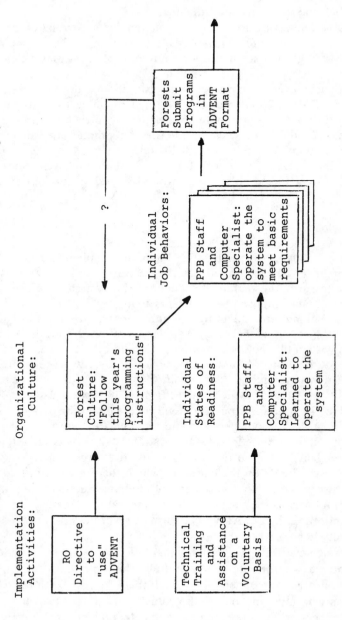

needed from the supervisor was a directive to follow the regional programming instructions for this year, which was normal practice.

The region's implementation strategy therefore had two parts. The first part merely consisted of directives to the forests describing the programming requirements for fiscal year 1980. The other consisted of voluntary technical training and assistance to enable the PPB staffs and computer specialists to handle the data conversions required. No attempt was made to determine or alter the attitudes of anyone on the forests, and no part of the strategy was addressed towards any of the forest management. If, on a particular forest, the supervisor (or other important manager) was interested in actually making use of the ADVENT capabilities, then that was all the better. The regional strategy, however, made no attempt to push the forests into other than the baseline level of use for the fiscal year 1980 planning effort.

Analysis of the implementation results clearly shows the shortcomings of this strategy. It did not deal with the attitudes of the forest supervisors, the very individuals whose participation is most critical to implementation success. Nor did the strategy involve any attempt to generally familiarize the forest management—district rangers and resource staffs—with the ADVENT-assisted process. Yet this familiarity too is a requirement for successful ADVENT implementation.

The overall impressions gained during interviews with forest personnel tend to support the conclusions suggested by the quantitative data analysis. Approximately two-thirds of the forests adopted less than the full ADVENT implementation. Management attitudes on these forests ranged from indifference to outright hostility towards the full site-specific project, ADVENT-assisted planning approach. One forest supervisor stated that he would "fight tooth and nail" to avoid having to use that approach. More typical, however, was a general lack of awareness on the part of the supervisor, rangers, and resource staffs that a new approach to program planning was being proposed. ADVENT, to them, was simply a detail in this year's program planning instructions, of concern only to the PPB staff.

Although the region's implementation strategy served a few forests well, it had drawbacks as far as most forests were concerned. A few forests did not make as extensive use of the system as they might had more training and support been forthcoming from the region. The fact that all nineteen forests were put on the system, even at a primitive level, meant that the amount of help the regional staff could give any one forest was limited.

On the other hand, management on a few forests was actually alienated by the experience with ADVENT during the fiscal year 1980 cycle. To them, ADVENT consumed a great deal of their resources (e.g., staff time, computer budget) for very little return. Not really understanding what ADVENT was or what it did, they only saw their staff spending many hours trying to get their program data into a computer system which had become a severe bottleneck. The fact that this problem was due as much to the overload on the computer system as to the staff's inexperience with ADVENT was lost on them.

To achieve full implementation of ADVENT on all forests in the future, Region 6 is going to have to eventually address the issues it chose to sidestep this first year. These are (1) what exactly is it they want the forests to do, (2) what roles does that imply for what individuals on the forests, and (3) how do they help equip those individuals to handle those roles. Programming personnel on the forests have repeatedly expressed concern over the lack of definition of management's role in the process. This concern was the dominant theme of a meeting held in June 1978 at the regional office to critique the just-completed programming cycle.

Despite the shortcomings in Region 6's implementation strategy, several forests, as shown in Figure 5-1, were relatively successful. If we examine the factor scores for these forests we find that they are very similar, and that they indicate the following conditions on the forests:

1. The forest supervisor was "sold" on the use of ADVENT; that is, he believed that ADVENT provided an advantage over the forest's previous method of program planning
2. The forest staff was aware of the forest supervisor's interest in using ADVENT, and believed that it was important to him
3. The program planning leader was skilled in using the ADVENT system
4. Someone on the forest was skilled enough in using computers to be able to run the system
5. The forest staff, usually through previous experience, was familiar with the process of preparing program plans using site-specific project data

This lends support to the first hypothesis: that success is, in fact, correlated with identifiable forest characteristics. The next step is to move from this explanatory posture to a normative one. Given that we know the prerequisites for ADVENT implementation success, we must now turn to formulating a strategy which will enable the forest to meet these prerequisites. This is what was attempted in NFS Region 3. Strategy formulation in Region 3 is the subject of chapter 7.

7

Strategy Formulation in Region 3

Introduction

NFS Region 3 (Arizona and New Mexico) began forest-level ADVENT implementations with the fiscal year 1981 program planning cycle. The regional PDB staff began to consider implementation strategy during the late winter of 1978.

Figure 7-1, a partial organizational chart of the regional office, shows the principal players at the regional level. M. J. "Jean" Hassell, the regional Forester, had had a long and varied career in the USFS. He started his career in Region 3, and had been a supervisor on one of the regions' forests, but had also seen service in other regions and the Washington Office. Hassell had long been interested in the study and practice of management, and had been cited in the early 1970s for his contribution to the development of the NFS's interdisciplinary approach to planning and decision making (Karder and Oglesby, 1973). Hassell was a forester by training, as were most NFS line managers.

Larry Coffelt, Director of Program Development and Budget for the region, had been manager of the USFS working capital fund in the Washington Office before joining the regional staff. He also was originally from Region 3, having served as budget officer on two Region 3 forests and in the regional office. Coffelt's college background had been in business administration. The fact that he reports directly to the regional forester, rather than to the deputy for administration (as is the case in some regions), attests to Hassell's feeling of the importance of program planning and budgeting.

Larry Medlock, the regional program analyst, was the individual who would be responsible for the detailed day-to-day management of the ADVENT implementations. He had served as administrative officer on two Region 3 forests before joining the regional staff, first as budget analyst and then as program analyst. Medlock was familiar with ADVENT from having used the system extensively in preparing the regional program

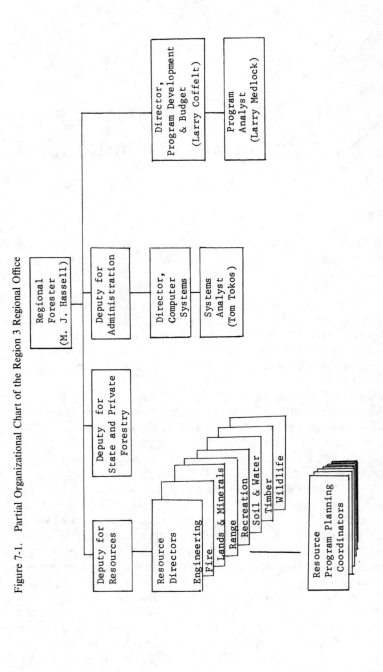

Figure 7-1. Partial Organizational Chart of the Region 3 Regional Office

Regional Forester (M. J. Hassell)

Deputy for Resources

Deputy for State and Private Forestry

Deputy for Administration

Director, Program Development & Budget (Larry Coffelt)

Program Analyst (Larry Medlock)

Director, Computer Systems

Systems Analyst (Tom Tokos)

Resource Directors

Engineering
Fire
Lands & Minerals
Range
Recreation
Soil & Water
Timber
Wildlife

Resource Program Planning Coordinators

proposals for fiscal year 1980. He also had a business administration degree.

Tom Tokos, regional systems analyst, would be responsible for computer support at the regional level, and training and assistance in the areas of ADVENT itself and the computer system in general. He had previously been computer specialist on a California forest which used ADVENT, and had supported the regional office use of ADVENT during the fiscal year 1980 programming effort.

Region 3 was beginning its ADVENT implementations in accordance with the Chief's directive that all forests be on the system by the fiscal year 1983 planning effort. Coffelt and Medlock decided from the first to phase the implementation effort over several years, implementing AD-VENT on several new forests each year. They felt that this approach would allow them to provide adequate support to the forests using the system for the first time each year. Additionally, they and the regional forester recognized that management on a few forests would be quite resistant to adopting this system. They felt that a multi-year implementation would help overcome this resistance. For one thing, as more and more forests in the region successfully used ADVENT, those resisting the system would come under peer pressure to implement it themselves. Also, they expected that transfer of personnel from ADVENT forests to the non-ADVENT forests would help pave the way for eventual implementation. Even if some forests never went on the system, the regional staff felt that first priority should be to help those forests which could and would try it.

This author met with Coffelt and the regional director of computer systems in early April 1978 to discuss the lessons learned in Region 6, and to suggest a way of approaching the implementations using the conceptual scheme which had been developed. An agreement was made to work together in analyzing the needs of the implementing forests and in developing implementation strategy, under the aegis of the Cooperative Study agreement. This meant that this author would act as a consultant to Coffelt and Medlock as they designed the implementation strategy and helped the forests execute it.

During the spring, the PDB staff developed a general timetable for the implementations:

1. Select the forests which would implement ADVENT this year by May 1978
2. Complete implementation strategy formulation by June
3. Carry out implementation activities needed to make the forests ready to begin using ADVENT by mid-September

4. Forests use ADVENT to prepare fiscal year 1981 program plans during the period from October 1978 to January 1979
5. Forests submit fiscal year 1981 program plans in early January 1979

This timetable was communicated to the forests selected for implementation in mid-May (see Appendix C, PDB letter of May 19, 1978).

Many of the region's forests had indicated a willingness to try AD-VENT during the fiscal year 1981 program planning effort. After discussions with the regional forester and his own staff, Coffelt narrowed the list to five possibilities. He felt that this would be the largest number that his staff could possibly support during this first cycle. These five forests were managed by supervisors who had professed an interest in program planning as a management tool. Coffelt and Medlock felt that, given this basic interest on the part of the supervisor, the forests could obtain the other necessary skills and attitudes through the implementation activities.

The list was further narrowed from five forests to three. One of the forests which volunteered was rejected because Medlock felt that the supervisor didn't really understand what ADVENT implied, but merely wanted to be on the bandwagon. He recommended that this forest be put off to a subsequent year. The other forest was rejected because its supervisor was well known to the regional staff as a "maverick" who insisted on doing everything his own peculiar way. Coffelt and Medlock finally decided that there was simply too much risk of this forest confusing the first year effort by going off on tangents of its own. They concluded that this unit could be better controlled in a later implementation cycle, once the ADVENT process had been well established in the region, and they themselves had had some practice in managing implementations.

Thus, three forests were finally selected—the Gila, Lincoln, and Kaibab. These forests were officially notified of their selection in late April (see Appendix C, PDB letter of April 28, 1978).

Definition of Goals, Behaviors and Desired Learning States

This first step of defining goals and behaviors was actually done in an iterative fashion over a period of several months. The original definition of the goals of the implementations grew out of a series of discussions between the regional forester and PDB director during the previous winter. The Chief had ordered that all forests be on the ADVENT system by the fiscal year 1983 planning cycle. In Region 3, the regional office itself had used ADVENT during the previous programming effort, but no forests were yet on it. For the fiscal year 1981 effort the forests were to start.

Hassell and Coffelt viewed the ADVENT system not as just another Washington-imposed requirement, but rather as an opportunity to improve the management of the forests. Hassell had a clear idea of how he wanted to control his forest supervisors—he wanted then to be able to propose and commit to a set of objectives against which he could then measure their performance. His goal was a control system in which the supervisors' performance was measured against real, quantifiable, and objective standards, so that the annual appraisals could be more than just (as he put it) "BS sessions". To him program planning was the natural process by which he and the supervisors would agree on these objectives. But there had been many problems in the execution of this process in the past.

Most disturbing were the continual changes in the programming instructions issued by the Washington Office each year. Forests complained that they spent more time figuring out this year's instructions than they did in actually preparing program plans. There was also an inconsistency between the formats of program plans and the work plans used for budget allocation and tracking during the target year. Because of the instability of the process, most forests prepared program plans at a much grosser level of detail than that which they used to allocate budgeted funds. This meant that when funds were allocated for the target year, the original program proposals were of limited use in preparing actual work plans.

Another problem was a lack of consistency across forests in the program data submitted. Both the regional forester and his staff realized that the accuracy of the proposals varied from forest to forest, according to the time and effort spent preparing them, and the personnel involved in generating them. This made it difficult for the regional forester to make trade-offs between forests in the allocation of discretionary funds. As a result of all of this, many forests felt that program planning was an exercise of doubtful utility, and treated it as such. To these forests, program planning was something to be taken care of with as little manpower as possible, since nothing substantive was likely to come of it. In a way, this was a vicious cycle: the less effort the forest put into programming, the less likely their program plans were to cause results, and therefore the less incentive they had to put effort into the process.

Both Hassell and Coffelt believed that putting an ADVENT-assisted program planning process in place on the forests could help solve these problems. By forcing the forests to use site-specific projects generated by the ranger districts as the basic program data units, they forced consistency both in the data itself and in the personnel involved in the process.

This also made the program planning format consistent with the budget allocation formats, so that much of the work done at program planning time would not have to be repeated at budget allocation. Projects which were generated for program proposals, and which were subsequently funded for execution, could be used as-is for purposes of budget tracking and attainment reporting.

The use of site-specific projects would also help lessen the impact of the Washington Office's yearly changes. Since the projects actually describe work that is done "on the ground" their definition is fairly stable. What goes on "on the ground" doesn't change that much from year to year. Coffelt thought that if the forests were generating proposals at this level of detail, then the regional office could extract from the data whatever it was that the Washington Office wanted this year. This would go a long way towards insulating the forests from procedural changes.

Thus the management of Region 3 defined a set of goals which went far beyond the basic need to meet the Chief's directive. In summary, these basic goals were (1) to put in place a process which was consistent across all forests, (2) to make it stable from year to year, (3) to integrate it into the management process, and (4) to make it efficient in terms of the manpower required. If the implementation could achieve these goals it would be considered a success by the regional forester and staff.

Once these goals were specified, a definition of the implementation itself (i.e., the events, activities, and outputs which were to occur on the implementing forests) could be made explicit. This definition was repeatedly refined during the spring and early summer of 1978. In deciding on the goals of the implementation, Hassell and Coffelt had specified some major features: the use of site-specific projects, and the ranger district involvement. This was further refined when this author presented the results of the Region 6 study in April. In late May, Coffelt, Medlock and this author spent a day in the regional office discussing the process and what features it should have. Finally, in early July, the supervisors of the implementing forests met with the regional staff to specify the last unsettled details and give their approval. The regional office, in a letter dated July 24 (see Appendix C), officially set forth this implementation definition, which can be summarized as follows.

The flow of events through a program planning cycle on a forest would begin with the supervisor's office staff issuing instructions and directions for the ranger district personnel as to the parameters of the program data they should prepare. Ranger district staffs would then generate their programs in the form of site-specific projects—that is, work projects which represented proposed activities to be performed in the district during the target year. These projects would be submitted to the supervisor's office staff for editing and entry into the ADVENT system. Using ADVENT, the forest staffs, with supervisor and ranger participation, would select and aggregate project data into forest program proposals. Both direction-setting and program formulation would of course involve negotiations between supervisor and rangers and between the various resource areas. Finally, the forest would submit the program proposals to the regional office.

This process as defined closely resembled what was considered successful ADVENT use in Region 6 the previous year. Hassell and Coffelt agreed that this was a process which (1) was applicable to all Region 3 forests, (2) could be used for program planning in future years with minimal change, and (3) would, in the long run, reduce the manpower impact of programming and budgeting.

During the session at the regional office in late May, the researcher and the PDB staff also attempted to identify the individual behaviors which were implied by the events, activities, and outputs specified for the implementation. (At this point, the implementation definition was not significantly different from what was finalized on July 10 and 11). Briefly, these were as follows:

1. *Forest Supervisor.* The supervisor must agree to use the system on his forest and issue the instructions to his personnel that they use it. He must also demonstrate to his subordinates that he intends to use the system as a decision-making aid.

2. *District Rangers.* The rangers must guide the use of the system on their district as their functional staff people put together site-specific projects. They should coordinate the process among their people so that viable district programs are formed from the various projects they submit.

3. *Ranger District Staff.* The staffs on the districts and the rangers must actually generate the bulk of the specific projects (including the number of people, resources, dollars, and equipment needed to accomplish a project), and record the information in the proper format.

4. *Supervisor's Office Staff.* The resource staff members in the supervisor's office have several responsibilities. They should advise the forest supervisor on the objectives and directions issued to the districts for programming. They should advise the ranger district personnel in their functional area when the program data is being generated. They should edit and validate the projects submitted by the districts in their particular area. Finally, they

should advise the forest supervisor during the process of forming forest programs from the projects.

5. *Program Planning Leader.* Someone on the supervisor's staff must manage the process, ensuring that deadlines are met, proper formats are used, technical assistance is made available, and so on. This person will also be responsible for editing and ensuring that the projects submitted by the districts are in the proper format. Further, this person is responsible for helping the forest personnel in using and interpreting the outputs from ADVENT.

6. *Computer Specialist.* This person will actually operate the computer facilities (intelligent terminals) in running the ADVENT programs. He will be responsible for problem solving and technical support in the areas of ADVENT itself and the computer system in general.

With each individual's behavior specified, the next step was to identify the knowledge, skills, and attitudes necessary to enable them to perform these tasks. Again, this was first explicitly considered in the May session in the regional office and then refined during the next two months as this author and the PDB staff worked with the forests.

Appropriate attitudes are most critical in the line management, who should commit to actually using the system as a management tool on the forest. Because of the fairly strong ethos of the Forest Service around authority, the line management (rangers, forest supervisors, and regional forester) must be predisposed toward assuming some personal responsibility for its success. This implies a positive attitude toward the system, not just a neutral one.

All personnel involved should have a basic knowledge of how the system works, but at varying levels of detail. For line management, knowledge of the capabilities of ADVENT and how it will be used in the management process will suffice. The staffs, who will be generating and validating project data, should be familiar with the formats and procedures and skilled enough at their use to be able to input data and request and utilize the reports. The program planning leader should be quite familiar with the technical details of the system, possess interpersonal skills for working with a variety of individuals on a new process, and have enough administrative skill to understand how to relate this process and system to the management process. The computer specialist should be knowledgeable in the basics of ADVENT itself and of computer-based systems as well. In short, there should be on the forest (1) management commitment to the process, (2) a general knowledge among the users of what they are doing and why, and (3) varying levels of technical, interpersonal, and administrative skills.

Measurement of Current States on the Forests.

The next step was to evaluate the current learning states and culture on the three forests selected for implementation. This was done jointly by this author and Larry Medlock, the regional program analyst, during early June 1978.

Each forest was visited for two or three days, during which interviews were conducted with the forest supervisor, all primary staff members, and most district rangers on each forest. The interviews explored each individual's role in the previous program planning efforts, his attitude towards program planning, his knowledge of ADVENT and computer-based systems in general, and any other pertinent subjects which arose. Basically the same information was gathered as was gathered on the Region 6 forests, except that more members of the forest staff were interviewed. In the sections below, each forest is described, especially as regards the assessment of their states of readiness to implement ADVENT.

Gila National Forest

The Gila (pronounced Hee'-la) National Forest, located in southwestern New Mexico, is one of the largest national forests in terms of land area—over 3.3 million acres. The main unit—just north of Silver City, site of the supervisor's office—forms an irregular outline about 65 by 100 miles in area. The Continental Divide meanders for 170 miles through this rugged canyon country which once was the stronghold of the Apache warrior Geronimo and his followers. Included within the forest boundaries are the 434,000 acres of the Gila wilderness, this country's first "official" wilderness area.

The lands of the Gila are very important to the economy of the surrounding area as a source of cattle forage. Over 30,000 head of cattle graze on the forest year-around. Recreation use, in the wilderness and in the forest itself, totals over 420,000 recreation visitor days annually. (A recreation visitor day is the equivalent of a person spending 12 hours on the forest in some recreation activity—camping, hiking, sightseeing, hunting, fishing, etc.) The Gila also produces a modest amount of commercial timber, with about 45 million board feet of softwood sawtimber being harvested annually.

To administer these and its other programs, the Gila's 1978 budget totalled over $7.9 million. The forest employed 283 persons (converting part-time employees to full-time equivalents) that year. Figure 7-2 shows the forest organization.

The Gila was one of the few forests in the region which already used site-specific projects in program planning. In fact, the process used on the Gila was similar in many respects to the desired organizational behavior defined by the region.

For fiscal year 1980 (the previous planning year) the Gila started the programming effort by assembling at the supervisor's office a team consisting of three rangers and the primary staff officers. This team took the programming directives issued by the regional office and developed from them (and forest goals and objectives) guidelines for the ranger district programs. Each district was required to submit three alternative programs representing different levels of funding.

The basic program data submitted from the districts was in the format of site-specific work projects. The programming team then used this data as the building blocks for the forest programs. This was a six week effort, which consumed much manpower in simple data handling. Finally, the forest programs were submitted to the regional office.

The line management commitment to and enthusiasm for this approach to programming on the Gila was remarkable. All of the rangers felt that they could, through program planning, influence what actually happened on their district. The fact that the Deputy Forest Supervisor acted as program planning leader attested to the high level of management concern for the process.

The primary task in implementing ADVENT on the Gila appeared from this to be one of equipping the forest to deal with the specifics of ADVENT itself. This includes codes and formats, features and capabilities, and operating procedures.

The only person on the forest with significant computer skills was the land management planner. Due to the demands of that function, forest management did not feel that he could take on responsibility for running ADVENT, although he might assist when possible.

Lincoln National Forest

The Lincoln National Forest comprises 1.1 million acres of mostly high country in southeastern New Mexico. The forest's location, atop mountain ranges surrounded by plains and desert, make it a popular recreation site for persons in southern New Mexico and west Texas. Recreation use, in both the forest and its 30,000 acre wilderness, totals 340,000 visitor days annually. About 12,000 head of cattle can be found on the forest's

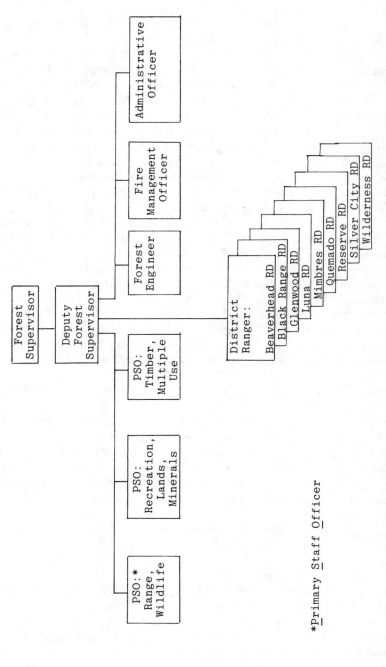

Figure 7-2. Gila National Forest Organization

*Primary Staff Officer

grazing allotments. The Lincoln's timber harvest is small, amounting to less than 7 million board feet of sawtimber per year.

The Lincoln's expenditures for fiscal year 1978 totalled approximately $5.3 million. During that year, the forest employed the equivalent of 246 full-time personnel. Figure 7-3 shows the forest organization.

In prior program planning efforts, the Lincoln had employed an approach which involved some forest-wide aggregates and some site-specific projects. The supervisor's office staff prepared forest wide aggregate programs representing all the ongoing work on the forest. The rangers and their staffs helped verify these programs, and added, in the form of site-specific projects, new development work they proposed on their districts.

The forest supervisor saw the advantage to preparing programs from site-specific data originated by the ranger districts. It was for this reason that he was actively seeking ADVENT implementation. He had an ally in the Forest Engineer, a highly motivated and analytical individual who understood the advantages of ADVENT.

Two of the four district rangers and two of the six primary staff officers were scheduled to be replaced before the fiscal year 1981 programming effort started. It was assumed for the purposes of implementation planning that their replacements would not be familiar with either the site-specific project approach to program planning or the ADVENT system. There was no computer specialist on the forest, nor did management feel that anyone in the existing organization could fill that role.

Kaibab National Forest

The Kaibab National Forest encompasses 1.7 million acres in northern Arizona surrounding the Grand Canyon National Park. The forest is one of the larger timber producers in the region, with an annual sawtimber harvest of 64 million board feet, one-fifth of the region's total. Its proximity to the Grand Canyon also brings it over 450,000 visitor days of recreation use annually. Its grazing allotments support approximately 8,000 head of cattle.

In fiscal year 1978, the Kaibab's budget totalled over $9 million, the largest of the three forests under study. During that year, employment on the forest was the equivalent of 238 persons full-time. Figure 7-4 shows the forest organization.

Of the three forests interviewed, the Kaibab showed the strongest supervisor's office staff influence in the programming process. Although the rangers and their staffs were involved in supplying some information, the actual program preparation was done along functional lines by the supervisor's office staff.

Figure 7-3. Lincoln National Forest Organization

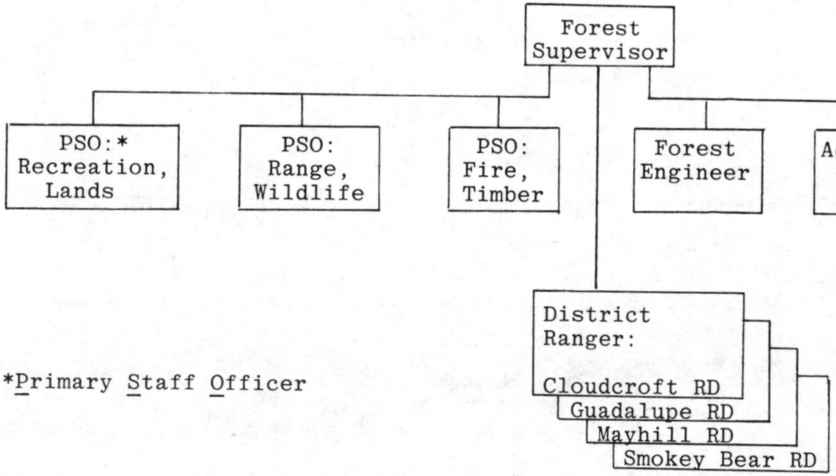

Forest Supervisor

PSO:* Recreation, Lands

PSO: Range, Wildlife

PSO: Fire, Timber

Forest Engineer

Administrative Officer

District Ranger:
Cloudcroft RD
Guadalupe RD
Mayhill RD
Smokey Bear RD

*Primary Staff Officer

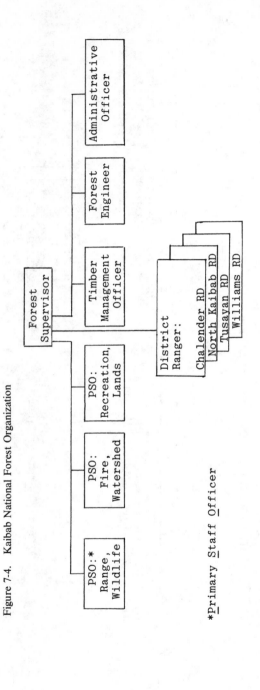

Figure 7-4. Kaibab National Forest Organization

Forest Supervisor

PSO:* Range, Wildlife

PSO: Fire, Watershed

PSO: Recreation, Lands

Timber Management Officer

Forest Engineer

Administrative Officer

District Ranger:
Chalender RD
North Kaibab RD
Tusayan RD
Williams RD

*Primary Staff Officer

Basically, each staff member was responsible for preparing the forest program(s) in one or more resource areas. To do this, the staff person would meet with personnel on each of the districts to identify district needs, project proposals, and unit costs. The staff person would then aggregate the district inputs and formulate forest program proposals for the resource area. The district rangers never saw a district program, either by resource area or overall.

The supervisor had been interested in going to ADVENT in order to establish a process which involved the rangers more. This would be, however, a process which would be quite new to both rangers and primary staff.

The rangers were not aware of the supervisor's reasons for wanting to adopt the process. They only knew that there would be a new wrinkle, called "ADVENT", in this year's program planning.

There was no computer specialist on the forest, nor was there anyone in the existing organization who could fill that role.

Summary of Current States

To summarize, we can view the three forests in terms of the factors determined in the study of Region 6 to be important to implementation success.

Factor 1: Familiarity of Management and Staff with the Process.

1. *Gila:* All forest personnel are quite familiar with the process of programming using site-specific projects.
2. *Lincoln:* Personnel who have been on the forest have some exposure to the process; a number of key individuals are new, however, and their experience is unknown.
3. *Kaibab:* No one on the forest is experienced in the site-specific project-based approach.

Factor 2: Supervisor commitment and demonstration of commitment.

1. *Gila:* Supervisor understands the process, is commited to it, and has repeatedly demonstrated that commitment.
2. *Lincoln:* Supervisor understands process and is committed to it; he has demonstrated his commitment to some forest personnel, but not all.
3. *Kaibab:* Supervisor understands and is committed to process; he

has not, however, effectively communicated this to forest personnel.

Factor 3: Program Planning Leader Familiarity with ADVENT.

1. *Gila:* No knowledge of ADVENT.
2. *Lincoln:* Forest Engineer, who assists as PPL, familiar with features and capabilities of ADVENT, but not operations.
3. *Kaibab:* No knowledge of ADVENT.

Factor 4: Computer Capabilities.

1. *Gila:* One staff member, whose availability is limitied.
2. *Lincoln:* None.
3. *Kaibab:* None.

Figure 7-5 sums up the status of the forests at this point. It is interesting to note that there were significant differences in the states of readiness among the forests, despite the fact that they had been picked as the "most likely to succeed" in the region. Only the Gila seemed, at this point, to be a "natural" for successful ADVENT use. If a Region 6 type of implementation strategy were used in Region 3 (i.e., only technical training on a voluntary basis), successful ADVENT implementation on the other two forests would be less than assured. The point of the tailored implementation strategy in Region 3, then, was to increase the likelihood of success on all forests.

After the forest visits in early June, this author and PDB staff met again in the regional office to consider implementation activitives. An outline of the implementation strategy was developed at this time.

Implementation Activities Prescribed

The implementation strategy consisted of four main elements:

1. Reinforced Management Commitment: a number of items would address this. The regional forester, in a letter and in a forest supervisors' meeting, stressed his interest in seeing ADVENT used by the forests. Visits would be made to a forest which had been using ADVENT successfully, so that forest management could have the system presented by one of their peers. Finally, the regional staff would have the three forest supervisors define many of the parameters of the process (such as exact project

Figure 7-5. Status of the Region 3 ADVENT Forests before Execution of Implementation Activities
(i.e., early summer, 1978)

Factor	Gila	Lincoln	Kaibab
Management familiarity with site-specific programming process	High	Moderate	Low
Supervisor commitment to the process	High	High	High
Supervisor commitment as perceived by rangers/staff	High	Moderate	Low
Program planning leader's familiarity with ADVENT	None	Moderate	None
Level of computer skill on forest	Moderate	Low	None
Probability of implementation success assuming a Region-6 type strategy	High	Moderate	Low

Figure 7-6. Region 3 ADVENT Implementation Strategy

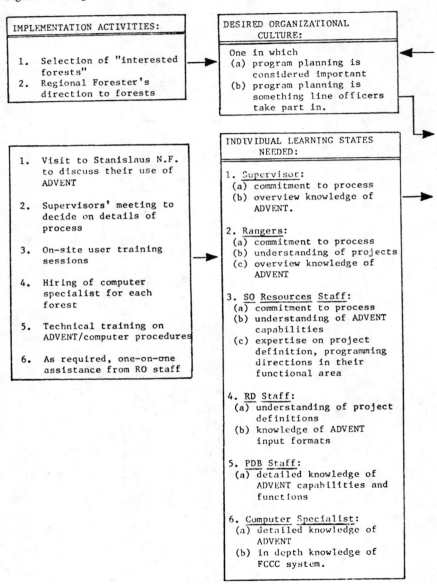

IMPLEMENTATION ACTIVITIES:

1. Selection of "interested forests"
2. Regional Forester's direction to forests

DESIRED ORGANIZATIONAL CULTURE:

One in which
(a) program planning is considered important
(b) program planning is something line officers take part in.

1. Visit to Stanislaus N.F. to discuss their use of ADVENT

2. Supervisors' meeting to decide on details of process

3. On-site user training sessions

4. Hiring of computer specialist for each forest

5. Technical training on ADVENT/computer procedures

6. As required, one-on-one assistance from RO staff

INDIVIDUAL LEARNING STATES NEEDED:

1. Supervisor:
   (a) commitment to process
   (b) overview knowledge of ADVENT.

2. Rangers:
   (a) commitment to process
   (b) understanding of projects
   (c) overview knowledge of ADVENT

3. SO Resources Staff:
   (a) commitment to process
   (b) understanding of ADVENT capabilities
   (c) expertise on project definition, programming directions in their functional area

4. RD Staff:
   (a) understanding of project definitions
   (b) knowledge of ADVENT input formats

5. PDB Staff:
   (a) detailed knowledge of ADVENT capabilities and functions

6. Computer Specialist:
   (a) detailed knowledge of ADVENT
   (b) in depth knowledge of FCCC system.

```
┌─────────────────────────────────────────────────────┐
│                                                       │
```

INDIVIDUAL JOB
BEHAVIORS DESIRED:

1. Supervisor:
   (a) mandate implementation
   (b) demonstrate commitment

2. Rangers:
   (a) mandate implementation
       on their districts
   (b) coordinate forming
       RD programs from
       project data

3. SO Resource Staff:
   (a) advise forest super-
       visor on objectives
       and directions for
       forest & RD's
   (b) advise RD personnel
       in their functional
       areas
   (c) validate RD project
       data
   (d) advise forest super-
       visor on putting
       together the forest
       program proposals

4. RD Staff:
   (a) prepare projects in
       accordance with
     · directions and in
       ADVENT format

5. SO PDB Staff:
   (a) manage the process
   (b) advise other forest
       personnel on ADVENT
       matters

6. Computer Specialist:
   (a) manage the computer
       facilities
   (b) advise on computer

DESIRED ORGANIZATIONAL
BEHAVIOR:

Forests develop program
proposals using
(1) Site- or district-specific
    projects;
(2) Ranger district
    involvement;
(3) ADVENT computer system
    to manipulate data

END GOAL:

Forest program planning
which is
    (1) stable
    (2) consistent
    (3) integrated
    (4) effective
    (5) efficient

definitions) so that they would be more likely to suit the forests' needs.

2. User Familiarization: this would aim at the rangers and staffs on the forests who would be the primary users of the system. This would be accomplished on-site at each forest, and would consist of three parts: (1) an overview and justification of the process presented by the forest supervisor; (2) instructions on project definitions, input formats, codes, and so on, presented by the forest program planning leader with regional staff assistance; and (3) instruction on ADVENT features and capabilities, presented by regional staff.

    This part of the implementation activities would be tailored to the individual forest. Sessions on the Gila would stress the details of the ADVENT system and how it differed from their existing process. On the Lincoln, more emphasis would have to be put on the process of generating site-specific projects and using them to put together forest programs. On the Kaibab, it would be necessary to spend more time justifying the process and "selling" it to the forest personnel before going into process details.

3. Computer Expertise: it was decided that it would not be feasible to train anyone on the forest staff to handle this job. Each forest would therefore be authorized to hire a trained computer-specialist from outside the organization.

4. Technical training: this would be provided primarily for the program planning leader and computer specialist, and would cover the details of operating ADVENT and the computer system. This would be provided basically by the regional systems analyst (Tokos), both through on-site visits and by formal training in the RO.

Figure 7-6 shows graphically the Region 3 implementation strategy in the format of the conceptual scheme. It should be noted that this strategy incorporated those implementation activities which the regional PDB staff had already laid out for the forests (and which are described in the PDB letter of May 19, 1978 in Appendix C). The execution of the strategy on each forest and the results are the subjects of the next chapter.

The Strategy in Retrospect

In retrospect, we can see that the implementation strategies designed in Region 3 were truly multifaceted. They combined a number of change techniques, including getting top management support, increasing familiarity with the system, peer evaluation and interaction, participative design, technical education, job redesign, and structural and attitudinal interventions. The implementation model served in this case as a tool for focusing the strategists' attention on the particular changes required. Once these had been specifically identified, the strategists then could (and did) choose from a variety of techniques to actually effect the changes.

In the next chapter we will follow the three forests as they carried out the implementation activities and used ADVENT to prepare the fiscal year 1981 program plans. We will analyze the results of their efforts in light of the implementation activities executed by each. Finally, in chapter 9 we will see what conclusions can be drawn from the Region 3 experiences and this study in general.

8

ADVENT Implementation in Region 3

Introduction

The Region 3 forests prepared for their ADVENT implementations during the summer of 1978, as they executed the strategies described in the previous chapter. In late summer/early fall they began to actually prepare the data for the fiscal year 1981 program plans, thus launching into AD-VENT use. This use culminated in April 1979 when they submitted to the regional office their 1981 program plans in the ADVENT format.

The Region 3 implementation strategy consisted of a number of elements:

1. Personnel from the prospective Region 3 ADVENT forests would visit the Stanislaus National Forest in California for a two day discussion and demonstration of ADVENT. The Stanislaus had been using the system successfully for several years, and could give the Region 3 persons a peer evaluation of its strengths and weaknesses
2. Each forest would formally appoint a member of the forest staff to act as Program Planning Leader for fiscal year 1981 planning, and this person would be responsible for managing ADVENT use on the forest
3. Each forest would establish a GS-9 computer specialist slot, to be filled as soon as possible, preferably by July 1, 1978
4. A meeting would be held between the regional PDB staff and management of the three forests to collectively decide on certain details of the process not yet resolved
5. A user training session (1–2 days) would be conducted on-site at each supervisor's office to familiarize the forest staff with the features and capabilities of ADVENT
6. The regional Systems Analyst would be responsible for training

the computer specialists on both ADVENT and the Forest Service's computer system

7. The regional PDB staff would provide close assistance to the ADVENT forests as required during the time the forests were using it to prepare their program plans

This chapter traces the experiences of each of the three forests as they prepared for ADVENT and actually used it. As we will see, each forest differed in the degree to which it was able to follow the planned implementation strategy, and in the degree of implementation success which followed.

ADVENT on the Gila

The Gila National Forest was the unit considered by both the regional staff and this author to be the most likely candidate for successful AD-VENT use. Robert Williamson (the supervisor) had, shortly after taking over the forest five years ago, established a forest-wide program planning process. In this process, the district rangers were responsible for preparing site-specific projects from which they built district program proposals. Teams of rangers then worked with the supervisor's office staff to build the forest programs out of the district proposals. The entire process was under the direct supervision of the Deputy Forest Supervisor, and was closely monitored by Williamson himself. It seemed that on the Gila AD-VENT would merely computerize an existing system.

Because of more pressing concerns, the Gila missed the first implementation activity, the May visit to the Stanislaus. This was not considered important, given the Gila management's high level of familiarity with site-specific project-based planning.

The Gila announced in early June that it had an opening for a GS-9 computer specialist. The position had been set up to report to the Land Management Planning Officer on the forest, who in turn reported to the supervisor. At the same time, Williamson reported to the regional office that the Deputy, R. L. Jourden, would be the Program Planning Leader as before. The Administrative Officer would serve as his assistant, along with the computer specialist.

The Supervisor, Deputy, and Administrative Officer from the Gila all attended the start-up meeting in the regional office on July 10 and 11. In this meeting, representatives of the three forests worked out many details of the ADVENT implementation (see Appendix C, letter of July 24). Williamson and Jourden contributed heavily in this meeting, particularly on project definitions. Having used site-specific projects for several years on the Gila, they were able to speak from experience as to the advantages and disadvantages of different approaches. Williamson also commanded respect as the senior forest supervisor present.

The user training class was held on the Gila on August 8 and 9 at the supervisor's office in Silver City. Attending were all district rangers and their primary assistants (usually the district Range Conservationist and perhaps the clerk). The supervisor's office staff was represented by all primary staff officers, as well as many of the substaff.

Originally, the plan had been for the regional staff (Medlock and Tokos) to prepare and conduct these sessions on the forests. During the weeks preceding them, however, the regional staff was tied up with other more pressing matters, so that they were not able to devote any time to preparation. When Medlock suggested delaying the training, however, all three supervisors elected to maintain the schedule and have the forest program planning leader run the session. The regional people would attend and contribute where appropriate, but it would be primarily a forest responsibility to set up and manage the session.

In retrospect, this appeared to be a serendipitous occurrence, since it forced the forest supervisor to play a more visible role, reinforcing his subordinates' perception of his commitment. On the Gila, Williamson kicked off the meeting and spent about forty-five minutes explaining why they were going to use ADVENT and what benefits he expected from it. He then turned the meeting over to Jourden, who conducted the bulk of the presentations. Medlock took the floor periodically when it was necessary for him to explain some point. Most of this first day was spent in going over project definitions and coding conventions. Finally, Tokos closed out the first day with a presentation of the reports available from ADVENT and how they might be used.

The second day of the training was devoted to coding practice projects in the ADVENT format. This was strictly a forest session, without regional staff participation (Medlock and Tokos had returned to Albuquerque). The forest also settled on a tentative schedule for the fiscal year 1981 program effort (see Figure 8-1).

During the remainder of August, Jourden and a team of three district rangers worked on developing the direction package to guide the districts as they started programming. This package, reproduced in Appendix D, was mailed out on September 11, formally starting 1981 program planning on the Gila.

The computer hardware for the Gila arrived at the supervisor's office in late September. Unfortunately, the forest had not yet been able to hire a computer specialist. This became a problem in mid-October, when the

Figure 8-1.   Gila National Forest Fiscal Year 1981 Program Planning Schedule, Presented at Ranger/Staff Meeting, August 9, 1978

FY 81 Planning Schedule	
Procedure and Direction	September 11
Districts and Units Building Projects	September 18
Staff Review and Consensus (week of September 18-22)	September 22
Input System	October 15
District & Staff Review, Corrections & Validations	October 30
Develop Forest Program	November 1
Line Staff Review and Approval	December 1
Submit to Regional Office	January 1

schedule called for key-entering the projects. From that point on the lack of computer skill began to cause delays in the Gila's schedule.

The computer specialist finally arrived in early November. His previous position had been with the Internal Revenue Service in Detroit, and he had never before had any exposure to the Forest Service. Thus he had to learn about the Forest Service, the Fort Collins Computer Center, and ADVENT itself before he could be of much use to the Gila. This involved several weeks of training, and it was well after the first of the year before he was very productive.

A further problem which hindered the Gila was severe flooding in the forest area during late November. Many roads and bridges washed out, one ranger station was cut off, and a number of backpackers were stranded in the Gila Wilderness. This preempted management time and attention for over two weeks, and the program planning decision meeting scheduled for early December was pushed back into January.

This January schedule was also slipped when the forest found that it did not yet have a clean project database with which to work. For one thing, the forest was still suffering from its late start in getting onto the computer. This was compounded by the fact that the Gila, with its nine ranger districts, had an exceptionally large number of projects which proved very time-consuming to edit and enter. Also, a coding scheme change required by the regional office had aggravated matters by forcing the recoding of many projects. As a result of all of this, by early February the Gila had still not completed building a clean project database which it could start to analyze. (The regional office had, however, extended to April the deadline for detailed program submission, so the forests still had two months to work on them).

When this author and the PDB staff (Coffelt and Medlock) visited the forest in February, the frustration level was high. Williamson complained long and loudly about how this year's program planning effort was a "step backwards" for the Gila. In most years, he said, the Gila would be finished programming by this time, and the rangers would have their approved plans in hand. So far this year, all they've done is put data into the system, with no worthwhile results to show for it. This was "losing credibility" for the process with rangers and staff, he claimed.

Coffelt and Medlock, aware that Williamson was given to occasionally blowing off steam, listened to his comments and then discussed the situation. In the course of the discussion, Williamson and Jourden agreed that their problems stemmed from two sources, neither of which was intrinsic to ADVENT. One problem was the late arrival of the computer specialist, which severely delayed the entire effort. In previous years, when projects were manually accumulated into programs, much of that work—although time-consuming—was clerical in nature, requiring no special skills. Now that the forest was committed to using the computer system to accomplish this, however, special computer skills were required to get these accumulations done—and the lack of these skills had created a bottleneck. Williamson agreed that this particular problem was going away now that the computer specialist was performing his functions.

The other source of disruption, the one to which Williamson most strenuously objected, was the change in the coding scheme initiated by the regional office. He said that the forest had gone ahead full speed generating and coding projects with the understanding that the codes agreed upon at the end of the summer were fixed. When the region, in response to a Washington Office requirement, had changed some of the codes, the forest had had to significantly recode many projects. This resulted in unnecessary manpower expenditures, frustration, and delays, according to Williamson. Coffelt and Medlock could only agree that the changes had been unfortunate, and say that in the future every effort would be made to "set" coding schemes throughout a planning cycle. For now, however, the Gila would just have to stop and fix its projects before going any further with ADVENT.

One final problem hindered the Gila's ADVENT efforts. In early March, the computer hardware went down and remained out of commission for two weeks. It was mid-March before the forest was able to use the system at all.

Finally, in the latter half of March and early April, the Gila got its process back on track and prepared the FY81 programs. By the end of March, all the projects had been edited and entered and the ADVENT reports were available. In early April, the team of rangers and staff began building the forest program proposals, and this work went very quickly with the aid of the ADVENT system.

The Gila was able to meet the region's program submission deadline in April. By that time, the computer specialist was fully trained and the forest staff was used to reading and interpreting the ADVENT reports. Jourden and Williamson were generally satisfied with the process as it was now functioning. They had gotten back to the point where, as Jourden liked to express it, "everyday's a holiday, and every night's New Year's Eve."

ADVENT on the Lincoln

Jim Abbott, supervisor on the Lincoln, had taken over the forest in the midst of its FY80 program planning effort and had immediately perceived the need for some sort of analytical tool. The forest staff was expending much manpower in preparing the program plans, but Abbott did not feel that the information gathered gave him what he needed to make trade-off decisions for the forest. Having heard of ADVENT, he began to look into the possibilities of using it on the Lincoln.

In his efforts, Abbott was aided by Jerry Adamson, the Forest Engineer. Adamson was a competant, motivated, and analytical individual who shared Abbott's interest in improving program planning on the forest. Adamson was sent to sit in on this author's first meeting with the regional staff in April, 1978, in which the Region 6 results were presented.

Abbott had already been convinced of the usefulness of identifying site-specific projects for program planning. To him, this type of planning was necessary because of the maze of environmental laws with which the forest had to deal. Only if projects had been formulated well in advance and passed through the review process, he felt, could the forest be assured of having feasible projects during the execution year. He had formulated a conceptual scheme of how projects should be identified, formulated, reviewed, and finally built into the program plans (see Figure 8-2). Thus, to him, ADVENT was a natural tool for handling the projects.

Reflecting his interest in ADVENT, Abbott himself went on the visit to the Stanislaus, along with his administrative officer and one district ranger. During the time between this author's visit to the Lincoln in early June and the July meeting in the regional office, Abbott worked on project definitions. As a result, he came to the July 10/11 meeting with a complete list of suggested project definitions, and this formed the basis for discussion in the meeting. Abbott was also a strong proponent in this meeting for setting up codes in such a way as to allow manpower planning by specific skill.

Figure 8-2. Lincoln National Forest Conceptual Scheme for
Project Generation and Review

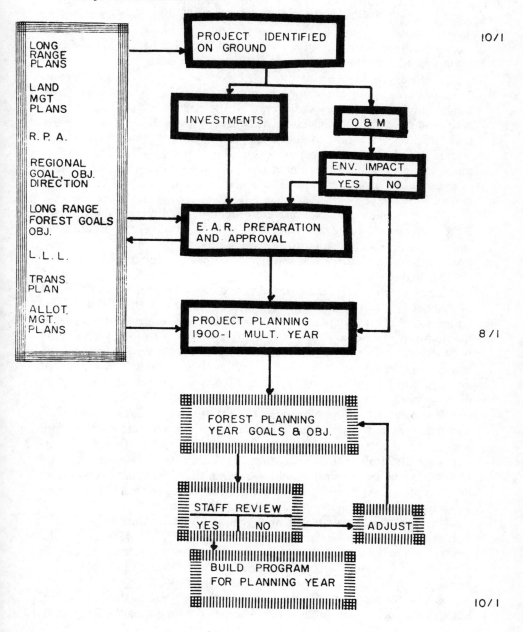

Formally, the Lincoln appointed the Administrative Officer as program planning leader. In practice, a team of several individuals carried out this role. The Forest Engineer and the Timber Management Officer (newly acquired from a Region 1 Forest which had used ADVENT) also worked with the Administrative Officer on ADVENT. Abbott himself very closely monitored the programming effort at all times.

The user training session on the Lincoln was held on August 10 and 11 at the supervisor's office in Alamogordo. Attending were all the district rangers and their primary assistants, all the supervisor's office primary staff, and much of the substaff. The first day was similar to that on the Gila, with regional staff (Medlock and Tokos) contributing where appropriate. The supervisor, forest engineer, administrative officer, and timber management officer all conducted parts of the program. Toward the end of the day, the class was broken into several groups for practice project coding.

The Lincoln's staff had already prepared the direction package for FY81 program planning (see Appendix D) by the time of this meeting, so the second day was devoted to reviewing this. At the end of this review, the rangers and staff were told to start preparing their projects for the FY81 programs.

The Lincoln's computer specialist had come on board about the first of August. He attended the user training session and then, since there was no ADVENT computer work yet to do, he was sent for a week to the Stanislaus National Forest to observe and learn about ADVENT. This proved quite effective, especially since he was able to obtain from the Stanislaus some programs for the intelligent terminal which facilitated entering and editing projects. When the hardware arrived on the Lincoln in September, everything was ready to start using ADVENT.

During October and November the various subunits (ranger districts and supervisor's office subunits) submitted their projects, which were validated and entered. Validation involved the appropriate functional staff checking the project for its information content (i.e., whether it made sense) and the administrative and computer staffs checking it for format and completeness. After this step the project would be turned over to the key entry personnel and keyed into the terminal's tapes.

Projects were accumulated on tape until all were complete in November, at which point they were entered into an ADVENT database on the central computer system. Initial reports were run, and a round of editing took place as obvious errors became apparent. Finally, in early December, a relatively clean project database was ready for analysis.

On December 12 the forest staff—rangers, their assistants, supervisor's office staff—met to begin the process of formulating the forest proposals. The goal of the meeting was to review the projects and come up with a minimum level program for the forest. (One of the alternative programs which the forests were required to submit was a base or minimum level program. This represented a level of funding and activity below which the forest could not fulfill its legally mandated functions. All the other higher levels were built on this base.) At this point, the supervisor's office staff (and Abbott) had had the various ADVENT reports for about a week. The rangers and their staffs were seeing the "live" ADVENT reports for the first time.

Each manager was given a set of reports on the projects for his subunit, including one showing unit costs by activity (e.g., dollars per acre of trees planted, per wildlife study undertaken, etc.). Abbott felt that going through these unit costs and comparing subunits would be a good way to hunt for further errors in the data. Accordingly, he started the meeting by having everyone look at these reports.

"Let's look at activity L22, trail rehabilitation," he started. "Mayhill shows $522 per mile for this, while Guadalupe has over $1500 per mile in L22. What makes these so different?"

Nobody answered. They had never been asked questions like this before, certainly not about program plans. Rangers and staff began flipping through the printouts, trying to find what Abbott was looking at, where the numbers came from. Gradually, the answers came out. For this particular activity, different districts had included different things under the activity code L22, and so the costs which resulted were not comparable.

As they worked through the unit costs, several sources of variability were uncovered. In some cases, differences in unit costs were legitimate, reflecting true differences in the environments of the districts. More often, they were due to inconsistency in coding the activities or interpreting the outputs, or to simple clerical error. Enough error was found that Abbott decided that the meeting should be adjourned so that everyone could correct their projects.

Even though the meeting had not met its original goal, Abbott and the regional staff were quite satisfied with what had happened. "This is what ADVENT is all about," one of them pointed out. In the past, all differences in costs between districts were attributed to environmental differences. Now, ADVENT was giving them a way to isolate the real, unavoidable differences in the costs of doing work among the districts. With this information, Abbott felt that he could make valid decisions as to where the forest's discretionary spending would be most cost-effective.

It was not until January that the rangers and staff met again to start formulating forest program proposals. This phase went very smoothly, however, and when this author and the RO staff visited the forest again in March, the programs were essentially completed. Discussions during that visit were mostly about the technical details of transferring the data to the regional office.

Medlock noticed that no one on the Lincoln had made much complaint about the regional office-required coding changes that had so troubled the Gila. When he asked about this, he found that although the Lincoln had also had to recode many projects, this had not been an overwhelming problem. With the administrative officer, forest engineer, timber management officer, and computer specialist all ADVENT "adepts", the recoding was simply taken care of in the supervisor's office and was not allowed to impact the rangers. The fact that the Lincoln was much smaller than the Gila, and therefore had fewer projects, also helped.

The Lincoln's satisfaction with ADVENT became apparent to the regional office and to the other forests in the region. Several times Abbott had used ADVENT reports to support a point he was making with the Regional Forester. In March, a team from the Lincoln visited another Region 3 forest, at that forest's invitation, to conduct an ADVENT briefing. Another Region 3 forest wanted the Lincoln's computer specialist to visit them and talk about ADVENT.

ADVENT on the Kaibab

The Kaibab National Forest had been chosen to be one of the ADVENT forests in large part because of the quality of the program plans it had submitted in past years and because of the general competance of the supervisor, Andy Lindquist. His interest in program planning as a management tool was proven, and the regional staff felt that this could overcome any problems caused by the forest staff's lack of familiarity with the site-specific project approach.

Lindquist saw program planning as a logical extension of land management planning, and felt that it was to be managed by the same person. Accordingly, the forest Land Management Planner was designated "Planning Officer" and put in charge of program planning as well. Because of his additional duties, he was made a primary staff officer, reporting directly to the supervisor. Previously, he had been a substaff member, reporting to the Administrative Officer. This Planning Officer was the only Kaibab representative on the Stanislaus visit.

The supervisor, Administrative Officer, and Planning Officer attended the July 10/11 session in the regional office. In general, their participation in the discussions was somewhat less than that of the other two forests. Lindquist himself took the position that detailed requirements should be kept as simple as possible in order to decrease the likelihood of foul-ups. He was in agreement, however, with those definitions and conventions which the group ultimately adopted.

The user training session on the Kaibab was held on August 17 at the supervisor's office in Williams. All the districts were represented by their rangers and one or two staff, and all primary staff members and many substaff from the supervisor's office were there. Again, Medlock and Tokos represented the regional staff.

The training was conducted by the Planning Officer, after Lindquist started the meeting by explaining why he had decided to go to ADVENT. Medlock occasionally took the floor to explain matters, and Tokos presented the ADVENT reports and their uses. A few practice projects were coded, and the program planning schedule for FY81 was presented (see Figure 8-3). Since the regional staff people had chartered a plane to fly to the meeting that morning and had to return the same evening, the session was limited to one day.

The districts and staff subunits began preparing projects in September. By mid-October Coffelt and Medlock were beginning to worry about the situation on the Kaibab. For one thing, the forest had been completely unsuccessful in its attempt to hire a computer specialist. The possibilities on the Civil Service rosters had been exhausted, to no avail. No one seemed to want to move to Williams, Arizona, as a GS-9. The prospects of getting someone in time to contribute to the FY81 program planning effort were growing dim.

Medlock also felt that there was a problem with the process management. The Planning Officer, he said, just didn't have the "horsepower" to make things happen the way they should. Having just been promoted from a substaff position in which he was not a manager, he had not yet acquired some of the managerial skills required for the program planning leader's job. As a result, rangers and staff were getting behind schedule and deviating from the standards in generating projects.

These deviations were to cause the forest problems when the region was forced to make its coding scheme changes. The regional office specified the new codes so as to minimize the impact on the ADVENT forests, assuming they were using the project definitions and codes agreed upon during the summer. For the Kaibab (which wasn't using all the agreed upon codes) the project reformulation which resulted was much more extensive than on the other two forests.

In early December Coffelt and Medlock discussed aborting the ADVENT implementation on the Kaibab for this year. The forest was falling further and further behind schedule in its programming efforts, and it

Figure 8-3. Kaibab National Forest Fiscal Year 1981 Program
Planning Flowchart and Schedule

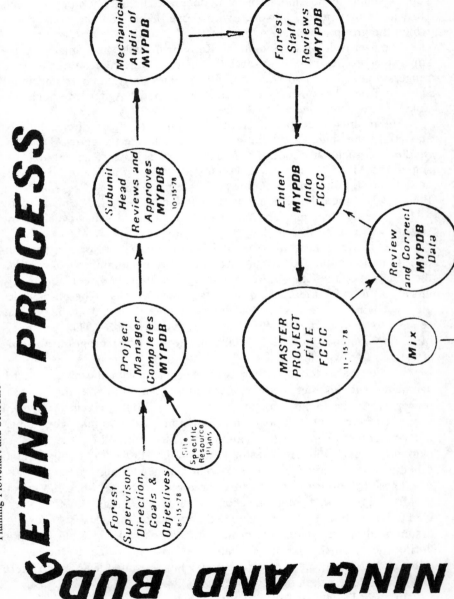

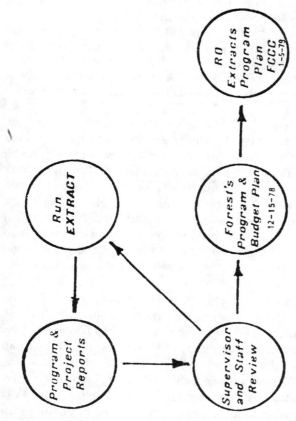

PROGRAM PLAN

seemed certain now that no computer specialist would be available for months. Tokos agreed to support the forest as much as possible from the regional office, but there were severe logistical problems with this. To reach Williams from Albuquerque, one either drove all day or flew to Phoenix, rented a car there, and then drove four hours to the supervisor's office. It was just not feasible to visit the forest very often.

Coffelt and Medlock finally decided that, despite the high risk of failure, the Kaibab should be allowed to continue. The forest had invested much effort in preparing the projects and if they were all thrown out now, they felt the negative reaction would be severe. They didn't, however, have very high hopes for success on the Kaibab.

Throughout the winter, the Planning Officer struggled to clean up and input the project data. Rangers and staff members began to complain about the ADVENT system, which had required much work but which produced no results. Medlock began to hear negative comments about ADVENT from other forests whose personnel had been talking to Kaibab staff.

By late February, Coffelt and Medlock were ready to write off the Kaibab's ADVENT efforts for FY81 planning as a loss. The forest seemed nowhere near even having a clean project database, much less running analyses. At the end of the month, Lindquist visited the Lincoln to talk with Abbott and, in his words, "to see what everybody was so damned happy about with ADVENT." Abbott and his staff explained how they were using the system and what it was giving them. Lindquist's reaction to this appeared noncommittal, but the Kaibab did continue its efforts to build a project database. Medlock continued to have frequent telephone conversations with the Planning Officer, answering questions and attempting to solve problems.

By late March, according to Medlock, things began to look surprisingly better on the Kaibab. Through sheer personal effort the Planning Officer had built the project database on the Fort Collins Computer System, and in early April was running ADVENT reports. The forest had also located a person on the regional engineering staff who was willing to transfer to the forest as computer specialist. He came on board in mid-April. This was too late to be of much help for FY81 planning, but it was a clear indication of the Kaibab management's commitment to stick with ADVENT.

The Kaibab finally succeeded in submitting their plans four weeks late, which, according to Medlock, was not a serious problem.

Summary

Figure 8-4 illustrates graphically the progress of the three forests through their ADVENT use in preparing the FY81 program plans. The difference between the Lincoln's implementation and those of the Gila and Kaibab is readily seen in this diagram. With computer skills available from the start of the programming cycle, the Lincoln very quickly arrived at the point where they could use the ADVENT reports. The longest part of their process (December through March) was their analysis phase, during which they used ADVENT to help formulate program plans.

Both the Gila and Kaibab show the effect of getting their computer skills late. The process on both these forests was drawn out during the time they were editing and key entering project data. They did not have anyone like the Lincoln's computer specialist, who could facilitate these steps through effective computer support. Thus the time available for analysis and management decision making on these two forests was relatively short.

This was less of a problem for the Gila than for the Kaibab. The rangers and staff on the Gila were already familiar with the process of building programs from site-specific projects, and they were able to formulate their programs quickly once the computer difficulties were solved. For the Kaibab, whose staff was new to the site-specific project-based programming process, the computer-related problems were enough to make them miss the regional deadline.

The Regional Office Perspective

"Well, we've sure learned something from this," was Medlock's evaluation of the ADVENT efforts on the three forests. "Our ideas about the necessary conditions for successful implementation were right on, and we got into trouble only where we didn't meet those conditions. From now on, these will be absolute requirements which must be met before a forest can even start to go to ADVENT."

Medlock was referring in particular to two prerequisites. One was the computer specialist—the experiences of the Gila and Kaibab had shown how necessary his skill was. The other requirement would be that a forest involve the ranger districts in program planning at least one year before going to the ADVENT-assisted process. Part of the problems on the Kaibab, he felt, stemmed from the rangers' and staffs' unfamiliarity with this programming approach.

These requirements were promulgated to the forests in a letter from the Regional Forester on April 4, 1979 (see Figure 8-5). Forests interested

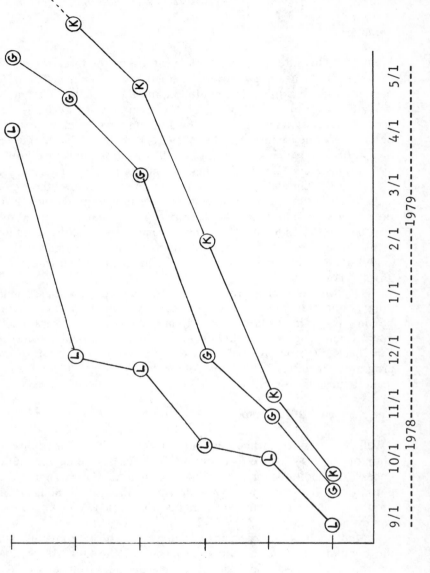

Figure 8-4. Milestone Activity Chart Showing Major Events as the Gila, Lincoln, and Kaibab National Forests Used ADVENT to Prepare Their Fiscal Year 1981 Program Plans
(Ⓖ = Gila; Ⓛ = Lincoln; Ⓚ = Kaibab)

in going to ADVENT were invited to attend a session in the regional office in which the Gila, Lincoln, and Kaibab would critique their FY81 process. However, no forest would be approved for ADVENT use until it could meet the requirements as stated.

Three forests (Santa Fe, Cibola, and Coconino) were able to meet the prior year planning method criteria, and indicated their desire to implement ADVENT for the FY82 planning cycle. These forests are currently working on the problem of acquiring a computer specialist. At least one other forest, at the time of this writing, had indicated in a letter that it was taking the steps necessary to enable it to use ADVENT for FY83 planning. Thus at least seven of the region's eleven forests were lined up for ADVENT implementation, and the region's long range plan appeared sound.

When asked to evaluate the success of the three ADVENT forests this year, Medlock was generally positive. Obviously the Lincoln was an unqualified success, and everyone from the Regional Forester on down knew it. The personnel on the Lincoln were quite satisfied with their process, and the forest was being used as a model of how ADVENT implementation should be carried off.

Medlock felt that the Gila, once they were over all their problems, had used the system effectively. Management on the forest was satisfied with the tool once they had gotten themselves into a position to use it properly. Medlock expected next year's planning effort on the Gila to go quite smoothly.

Most surprising to Medlock (and to this author) was the final outcome on the Kaibab. Although most of the FY81 effort on that forest had been time-wasting and frustrating, they had apparently struggled their way through to the point that they saw long term benefit from the system. At least they were willing to try it again the next year, and were expecting much better results.

Regional management was also basically satisfied with the ADVENT results. Hassell agreed with the PDB staff evaluations and recommendations concerning further ADVENT implementations. He even invited the Washington Office PDB group to send a representative to the FY81 critique session to learn from the Region's experiences (see Figure 8-6).

In the next, and final chapter, we will see what conclusions can be drawn from the Region 3 ADVENT implementations. That chapter will also address the overall conclusions of this study.

Figure 8-5. Letter from the Regional Forester, April 4, 1979

UNITED STATES DEPARTMENT OF AGRICULTURE
FOREST SERVICE

R-3

_____

PLY TO: 1930 Program Development and Budgeting   April 4, 1979

SUBJECT: Modified ADVENT Review and Training

TO: Forest Supervisors

Reference is made to the Modified ADVENT session identified in the
Calendar of Region Three Training Courses for May 15 and 16, 1979.

The Forests currently using the ADVENT computer software system are
requested to attend (Gila, Kaibab, and Lincoln National Forests).

Forests who have indicated a desire to use the ADVENT system are
invited to attend (Cibola, Coconino, Coronado, and Santa Fe National
Forests). Currently our assessment of the Region's and Fort Collins
Computer Center capabilities indicate only two or three of the four
Forests will be able to implement ADVENT for F.Y. 1982 program
planning.

Our experiences in the use of ADVENT for the F.Y. 1981 program
planning have been helpful in identifying specific system requirements. Therefore, the criteria this office will use in
selecting the next group of Forests to complement the system is:

    1. The Forest Supervisor must make the decision. The use of
ADVENT is not mandatory at the Forest level in this Region.

    2. The Forest process for F.Y. 1981 planning must have included
the District Rangers submitting projects using MIH codes to the
Forest Supervisor.

    3. The Forest must have the necessary computer hardware and a
Computer Specialist on board by August 30, 1979.

    4. The Deputy Forest Supervisor or a primary staff officer must
be assigned the direct management of the process.

    5. The Forest Supervisor must attend the May 15 and 16, 1979,
modified ADVENT session.

We plan to implement the ADVENT system on the remaining Forests that
wish to use the system for the F.Y. 1983 program planning effort.

Figure 8-5 (cont.)

2
1930-Forest Supervisors- 4/4/79

The objectives of the May 15 and 16 session are:

    1. · The Forests currently using ADVENT (Gila, Kaibab, and Lincoln National Forests) to examine the F.Y. 1981 planning. This will be an indepth critique of the Regional program planning process, Forest process, and the ADVENT computer software support to the processes.

    2. Using the critique of F.Y. 1981, discuss alternatives to improve the Region and Forest process for F.Y. 1982. Forests considering using the ADVENT computer system for F.Y. 1982 planning (Cibola, Coconino, Coronado, and Santa Fe National Forests) to benefit from the current ADVENT system Forests' experiences and suggestions.

The review will be held in the Regional Office, conference room 6008, starting at 8:00 a.m. on May 15, 1979. The Forest Supervisor and the Forest Program Planning Staff Officer should attend.

M. J. Hassell
M. J. HASSELL
Regional Forester

cc: Deputy Regional Foresters
     Resources Staff Unit Directors
     Administrative Management
     Coordinating Team Members

Figure 8-6. Letter from the Regional Forester Inviting the
Washington PDB Group to Send a Representative to
the Fiscal Year 1981 Critique Session

UNITED STATES DEPARTMENT OF AGRICULTURE
FOREST SERVICE

R-3

REPLY TO: 1930 Program Development and Budgeting

APR 10 1979

SUBJECT: Modified ADVENT Review and Training

TO: Chief

The detailed F.Y. 1981 program budget was developed on the Gila,
Kaibab, and Lincoln National Forests using the ADVENT computer
software to support the process. This was our first year to use
ADVENT at the Forest level.

On May 15 and 16, 1979, we will examine indepth the ADVENT system
implementation and application on the above mentioned Forests.
Based on this review, alternatives to improve the Region and
Forest level process for F.Y. 1982 planning will be developed.

Forest Supervisors who are considering using the ADVENT system for
F.Y. 1982 planning, as well as the Forest Supervisors currently
using the system, will be present. As part of the Harvard Business
School Cooperative Study, Mr. Lee Gremillion has been invited and
has agreed to attend.

We feel it is most important that a representative from your office
be available to assist us in this session. It is our request that
you make Mr. Bob Gordon, Program Development and Budget, available.

The session will start at 8:00 a.m. on May 15, in this office.
Additional information is contained in the enclosed copy of the
letter sent to Region Three Forest Supervisors.

M. J. HASSELL

M. J. HASSELL
Regional Forester

Enclosure

LJMedlock:bcm:4/9/79

Copy to Lee Gremillion
Harvard Business School
sent 4/11/79 bcm

9

Conclusions

Recapitulation of the Research Structure

The overall purpose of this study was the exploration of the usefulness of a systematic approach to formulating implementation strategy. A conceptual scheme was proposed as a framework for considering strategy formulation, and an action research program undertaken which made use of it. First, one group of units (Region 6) was observed and measured as it implemented the computer-based system (ADVENT). Then, based on insights gained from this observation, implementation strategies were systematically formulated using the conceptual scheme for a second group of units (Region 3). The results of these implementations were likewise observed.

Two hypotheses were put forward in conjunction with this research. The first of these suggested that implementation success would be correlated with identifiable characteristics of the implementing units. This hypothesis was addressed by the analysis of the ADVENT implementations in Region 6. As pointed out in chapter 6, definite positive correlations existed between the forests' success with ADVENT and certain critical knowledge, skills, and attitudes (KSAs) among various members of their management.

In formulating implementation strategy in Region 3, an explicit and systematic effort was made to foster these seemingly necessary KSAs on the implementing forests. The regional staff carefully defined the type of ADVENT use which would be "successful" in meeting regional management's objectives. From this they identified the role each member of the forest's management and staff must play, and the KSAs necessary for him to do so. Each forest was measured to determine its current status. Once this was accomplished, the regional staff ordered implementation activities specifically designed to strengthen weaknesses in the KSAs of the forests' management and staff.

The results of the Region 3 ADVENT implementations shed further light on the first hypothesis regarding the correlation between success and forest characteristics. More importantly, they address the second hypothesis, i.e., that the likelihood of implementation success can be increased through a strategy which attempts to supply or reinforce those characteristics.

Thus, the Region 3 results must be analyzed from two points of view, first as they reflect on the conclusions drawn from the Region 6 study, and then for their implications for the second hypothesis. Finally, we will step back and regard the Region 6 and Region 3 experiences as a whole, and see what conclusions can be drawn for practitioners considering implementation management.

Prerequisites for Implementation Success

The Region 6 observations suggested that there were four characteristics of the forest which successfully implemented ADVENT. These were:

1. Management commitment to the process and demonstration of that commitment
2. Forest staff understanding of site-specific project-based, ADVENT-assisted program planning
3. Capable process leadership which was skilled in the use of the ADVENT tool
4. Technical computer skill on the forest staff

The Region 3 strategy attempted to ensure that each forest met these conditions, either through forest selection or through implementation activities. In light of the implementation results reported in chapter 8, we can reevaluate each of these.

Management commitment. The Region 3 results seem to underscore the importance of this factor. This is especially well illustrated by the case of the Kaibab. Very little went right during most of that forest's ADVENT implementation, and aborting the effort could have been easily justified. Yet the forest supervisor didn't lose sight of his original goal in going to the system, and recognized that the problems they were having were soluble. As a result, the Kaibab continued its effort and finally appeared to overcome the problems which had been a hindrance (lack of computer skills, program planning leader inexperience). Although the FY81 ADVENT effort was hardly an unqualified success, the forest seems well prepared for successful use in following years.

This was also true on the Gila, where computer-related problems hindered their efforts. There was never any question about giving up on that forest, however. Everyone on the forest understood Williamson's reasons for going to ADVENT and understood that the implementation would be carried through. They recognized the problems they were having as temporary, "start-up" difficulties. Once they were able to work the computer properly, they proceeded with their implementation along the desired lines specified by the regional staff.

On the Lincoln, Abbott's enthusiasm for ADVENT contributed to the considerable success of that forest's effort. This interest and enthusiasm created an environment in which several members of his staff could and did actively involve themselves in making the system work. With this kind of resource devoted to it, ADVENT worked very well indeed on the Lincoln.

As in Region 6, management commitment was the key to success— the supervisor on the implementing forest had to believe that ADVENT offered him something of value. Interestingly enough, it appears that the three supervisors in Region 3 each had a slightly different reason for believing in the value of ADVENT. Williamson on the Gila saw it as an efficient means of automating that forest's existing, sophisticated program planning process. Abbott on the Lincoln was motivated more by the need to define and review projects far enough ahead of time to be able to meet the environmental analysis requirements. Lindquist on the Kaibab saw the ADVENT process as a tool for getting more district ranger involvement in program planning.

This suggests that the participative design aspects of the region's implementation strategy were of major benefit. The overall outline of the ADVENT process had been set by the need to meet the regional forester's objectives. Within that framework, however, there remained considerable flexibility to specify process details. The regional staff took the position that the implementing forest supervisors should be given the opportunity to define these details of the process so as to better meet their own needs. This was done in the meeting of July 10/11. Because of the supervisors' participation in the design, the process which resulted met the differing needs of the three forests, even though the process itself was a standardized one.

Forest staff familiarity with the process. The two forests which had implementation problems shed light most directly on this factor. The rangers and staff on the Gila were quite familiar with the site-specific project-based approach to program planning, having used it for several years. They recognized ADVENT as a computer-based tool which merely automated much of the data handling they had previously done manually.

Thus, when they had computer-related problems, everyone understood the cause and did not question the validity of the underlying process. When the computer-related problems were finally solved, the forest staff quickly and efficiently resumed the process and carried it to a successful conclusion.

The Kaibab's FY81 process, on the other hand, in addition to using ADVENT, was forcing the ranger districts to prepare and submit project data for the first time. The underlying process was new, as was the computer-based tool for automating it. When problems arose, some members of the district and supervisor's office staffs mistakenly interpreted them as intrinsic to the new process. They only knew that last year, when the supervisor's office staff did the programming, everything went smoothly. This year, when they themselves were having to spend much time and effort coding up projects, nothing was coming out of it. Even when the forest finally did get the system working, some rangers continued to feel that it was more trouble than it was worth. These negative reactions will have to be dealt with by forest management in next year's program planning.

The regional staff concluded that before implementing ADVENT, a forest should already be using the underlying site-specific project-based program planning approach. Accordingly, the regional forester, in a letter of April 4, 1979 (see Figure 8-5), advised the non-ADVENT forests that, in order for them to use ADVENT for FY82 planning, "the forest process for F. Y. 1981 planning must have included the District Rangers submitting projects using MIH codes to the Forest Supervisor."

Process leadership. Process leadership was strongest on the Lincoln, where four competant, motivated staff members (Administrative Officer, Forest Engineer, Timber Management Officer, and Computer Specialist) teamed together to make the process run smoothly and efficiently. The effect of this was best illustrated by the incidents in which the regional office changed some coding rules in the middle of the process. These changes caused frustration and complaints on the Gila and Kaibab, but were taken in stride by the Lincoln. The leadership team quickly identified the necessary modifications to the data and made them without impacting the line management.

Conversely, the regional staff felt that the inexperience of the Kaibab's program planning leader contributed to their problems during the early part of the process. Fortunately, that individual appears to have learned enough from the experience to have become more effective. Nevertheless, the regional staff felt that the need for a strong process leader was important enough that the Regional Forester's letter (Figure 8-5) reiterates it: "The Deputy Forest Supervisor or a primary staff officer must be assigned the direct management of the process."

Technical computer skill. The single biggest problem encountered in the Region 3 ADVENT implementation efforts was the difficulty in getting computer specialists for the forests. This lack of technical capability severely impacted the Gila's ADVENT use, and almost scuttled the Kaibab's implementation. Conversely, the strong computer specialist on the Lincoln was a key contributor to that forest's success.

The Region 6 data had indicated only a weak relationship between the level of computer skill on a forest and its ADVENT success. In retrospect, it seems that this was due to the fact that all the Region 6 forests had at least a modicum of computer skill. On all forests, this was enough to handle the baseline ADVENT implementation. Thus the variability of the data in this area was limited.

The Region 3 forests, on the other hand, being generally smaller than their Region 6 counterparts in budget and personnel, had little or no computer skill on their staffs. Also, they were all attempting much more than the Region 6 baseline ADVENT use. Thus they needed to have computer skill specifically supplied in order to use ADVENT successfully. When this was attempted, the forests found that a "seller's market" existed for persons with computer training, and that obtaining such a person would take considerable time—too much time for the Gila and Kaibab.

In order to avoid this situation in the future, the regional staff decided that forests must acquire their computer specialists before they start working with ADVENT. Accordingly, the Regional Forester's letter set the following requirement for forests wanting to implement ADVENT for FY82 planning: "The Forest must have the necessary computer hardware and a Computer Specialist on board by August 30, 1979."

One must conclude that the prerequisites for implementation success suggested by the Region 6 observations are supported by the Region 3 experiment. The strategy there consciously attempted to enable the forests to meet these prerequisites. Where they were able to do so, their implementations were successful; where they were unable to meet the prerequisites, implementation difficulties followed.

Managing the Implementation Process

The extent of ADVENT implementation success had been defined for the purposes of the experiment as the extent to which the actual system use on the forest was congruent to the desired system use envisioned by the

Regional Forester. In Region 3, this desired process of using the system involved five elements:

1. The Forest Supervisor and staff would provide programming guidelines for the District Rangers
2. Ranger districts would prepare site-specific projects in accordance with the guidelines
3. The projects would be built into an ADVENT database
4. The forest management team would analyze the data and formulate forest program proposals
5. The forest would submit its program proposals to the regional office in the form of an ADVENT database

Technically, each of the three forests accomplished all of the steps listed above (the Kaibab is currently performing the last one). Technically, then, one could claim implementation success for all three forests. By such a standard, we would have to conclude that the systematic management of the implementations was, in fact, successful.

Perhaps a more useful way to evaluate the forests' success is to then ask the question, from the Regional Forester's point of view, "Do we want other forests to implement ADVENT the way it was done on this forest?" In the case of the Lincoln, the answer would be a definite "yes". And, in fact, a description of the Lincoln's implementation has been circulated to all Region 3 forest supervisors as an example of what they should expect to do if they want to use the system themselves. By any set of standards, we would have to term the Lincoln's ADVENT implementation a success and conclude that it offers support to our second hypothesis.

We would not, however, want another forest's implementation to follow exactly the pattern set by the Gila or Kaibab. Both of those forests experienced periods of frustration and dissatisfaction before they were able to properly use the system. But if we look at the causes of these problems, we see that they stem from the *execution* of the implementation strategy, not from its *design*.

The regional staff recognized from the beginning the necessity of providing the forests with technical computer skill. What they didn't recognize was the difficulty they would encounter in obtaining that skill. It was no surprise that the Gila and Kaibab would have problems trying to use the system without a computer specialist—that was why they were authorized to hire such a person in the first place.

Despite their problems, both of these forests pulled through so that their long-range success in using the system seems likely. This suggests that the overall implementation strategy formulated by the regional staff was sound—the implementing units were able to survive one or two flaws in its execution. The three ADVENT forests in Region 3 provide too small a sample to allow any meaningful statistical evaluation. On an intuitive basis, however, their experiences appear to support our second hypothesis. In Region 6, where the implementations were basically unmanaged, there were a number of definite failures. By the standards which were used to evaluate the Region 6 ADVENT implementations, ADVENT use on the Lincoln, Gila, and Kaibab would have to be classified as quite successful.

Perhaps the best indicator of the success of the implementation management in Region 3 is its continued use in that region. The staff is certainly "tuning" their strategy to reflect the lessons learned this year, but the basic design is the same. In his letter of April 4, 1979, the Regional Forester gave his stamp of approval to the process.

Some Final Thoughts

When this research project was first formulated, the goal was to test the usefulness of the particular implementation scheme proposed in chapter 3. This author felt that this could provide a tool with which to "model" an implementation so that more effective strategies could be selected. The Region 3 experiment was specifically conceived to test the use of this scheme.

The use of this conceptual scheme in Region 3 was, in fact, quite helpful. This author and the regional staff found it to be a convenient device for "packaging" the different implementation elements into a neat whole. During the course of the experiment, however, it became apparent that, while the conceptual scheme was useful, it was not critical. The critical element was the fact that regional management was consciously attempting to increase the likelihood of implementation success by modifying knowledge, skills, and attitudes on the forests. They were assuming the responsibility for making the implementations successful. This was the key difference between the two regions studied.

In Region 6, the responsibility for using ADVENT effectively rested on the forests themselves. Further, the forests were responsible for determining whether they were capable of using it effectively, and if not, what they should do to acquire that capability. The analysis reported in chapter 6 showed that for many forests these were impossible tasks.

In Region 3, regional management took the basic position that they did not want to have a forest using ADVENT unless the forest used it correctly. Thus they defined what constituted correct use, evaluated what the forests needed to achieve correct use, and took steps to fulfill these needs. Responsibility for initiating and managing these activities rested upon regional management.

In retrospect, it seems that this conscious assumption of responsibility by the organizational superior is the key to success in a mandated implementation. The organizational superior orders the implementation because he sees a need which the system can satisfy. The implementing units themselves may or may not perceive this same need. Thus, they may or may not use the system in such a way as to address that need. Certainly there were forests in Region 6, for example, whose ADVENT use for FY79 program planning was an exercise which achieved no one's goals, neither theirs nor regional management's.

Only the organizational superior mandating the implementation is in a position to evaluate the gap between current and desired knowledge, skills, and attitudes on the implementing units. It may not be possible for the management and staff of a forest, for example, to know that they don't know enough about ADVENT before attempting to use it. The basic purpose of implementation activities is to bridge this gap. Specifying the implementation activities, therefore, must primarily be the responsibility of the superior mandating the implementation.

This is not to say that the proper way to implement standardized systems is through some sort of "power-coercive" intervention strategy. Rather, this study indicates that success is most likely when a partnership exists between implementing unit and superior, with the superior assuming the leadership role. As we have seen, assessing the current states of knowledge, skills, and attitudes on the implementing units is a critical step in formulating implementation strategy. This can only be done effectively if there exists a degree of openness and trust between superior and subordinate which allows free communication.

This "partnership" between regional office and ADVENT forests greatly facilitated the implementations in Region 3. The regional staff was initially familiar enough with the forests to be able to select the proper three for ADVENT use. They had free access to all forest personnel to evaluate their current states of readiness. An atmosphere of mutual understanding and trust enabled the forests to participate freely in the design of the process, and enabled the regional staff to recommend implementation activities with the knowledge that the forests would not resist them. Finally, as the forests encountered problems in using ADVENT, their reaction was not to blame the regional office for their difficulties but, rather, to turn to the staff for help in finding solutions.

This Region 3 experience also illustrates how the human and organizational aspects of implementation dominate the technical system aspects. ADVENT itself is a far from perfect tool. The Harvard team has repeatedly made suggestions for design changes in the system. It is badly documented, and awkward and inefficient to use in many ways. Yet these shortcomings of the system were not a factor in the Region 3 implementations. The system, flaws and all, was taken as a "given" which, on the whole, was considered worth using. The strategy was designed to enable the forests to use it as is; and, in fact, they were able to successfully use the possibly flawed tool.

Appendices

Relative Advantage Questionaire

                    POSITION_____
NAME_____   FOREST_____

We would like to know your expectations concerning the
use of ADVENT in developing the FY '80 program budget.
Please answer the questions from the point of view of
your   own forest, keeping in mind the personnel,
experience, and situations which are unique to your
organization.

1. What benefits do you expect your forest to realize
from using ADVENT? Check the most important.

2. What problems do you foresee in implementing ADVENT
on your forest? Check the most critical.

3.   What, if any, advantages of your current approach to program planning do you think you might lose by using ADVENT instead?

Please rate ADVENT against your forest's current approach to program planning and provide your own evaluation of the importance of the following characteristics.

4.   Ability to produce accurate costs and related outputs in program plans.

      1.   Current method far superior

      2.   Current method somewhat superior

      3.   Current method slightly superior

      4.   Both about the same

      5.   Advent slightly superior

      6.   Advent somewhat superior

      7 .   Advent far superior

5.   How important are highly accurate costs and related

outputs in program planning?

      1.   Extremely important

      2.   Very important

      3.   Somewhat important

      4.   Slightly important

      5.   Unimportant

6. How much impact does the program plan have in determining actual funding level (in your opinion)?

      1.   Plan totally determines funds

      2.   Plan very significan

      3.   Plan has some impact

      4.   Plan has slight impact

      5.   Plan has no impact

7. How would ADVENT implementation affect your forest's ability to obtain requested funds?

      1.   Current method far superior

      2.   Current method somewhat superior

      3.   Current method slightly superior

      4.   Both about the same

      5.   ADVENT slightly superior

      6.   ADVENT somewhat superior

      7.   ADVENT far superior

8. Funding considerations aside, how would ADVENT implementation affect the quality of forest planning, management, and operations?

1. Current method far superior
2. Current method somewhat superior
3. Current method slightly superior
4. Both about the same
5. ADVENT slightly superior
6. ADVENT somewhat superior
7. ADVENT far superior

9. What is your estimate (roughly) of the number of man months of effort which your forest put into preparing the FY '79 program plans? _____

10. How do you feel that this effort would have been affected had you used ADVENT?

1. Much longer with ADVENT
2. Somewhat longer with ADVENT
3. Slightly longer with ADVENT
4. Either about the same
5. Slightly longer with current approach
6. Somewhat longer with current approach

7. Much longer with current approach

11. Overall, considering all costs and related
benefits, how would you rate ADVENT against your
present approach?

1. Current method far superior

2. Current method somewhat superior

3. Current method slightly superior

4. Both about the same

5. ADVENT slightly superior

6. ADVENT somewhat superior

7. ADVENT far superior

12. Any other comments you might have?

Thank you very much for your help!

Forest Supervisor Questionaire

_____ Supervisor, _____ N.F.

1. Your opinion on the importance of PPB in

    a. obtaining funding:

    b. other:

2. Your opinion of your DR'S opinion of PPB
importance.

3. a) Did the forest use site-specific projects for FY
79?___ FY '80 ___

    b) Your opinion on the relative merits of
site-specific vs. unit-wide planning.

c) Supervisor's opinion of DR'S opinion on relative merits of site-specific planning.

4. What would be the impact of using ADVENT with site-specific projects?

a) on man-hours expended

b) on technical capabilities

c) on the accuracy of the program plan

d) other impacts

5. How large a change would site-specific ADVENT implementation make to the following individuals'

participation in the PPB process?   Good or bad?

   a) District Rangers

   b) SO Resource Staff

   c)   SO PPB Staff

   d) Forest Supervisor

   e) Anyone else

6.   Would site-specific ADVENT implementation cause changes in the following area?   Good or bad?

   a) Organizational structure

b) Decision making process

c) Manning level

7. Do you think that the PPB process is a priority issue with the Regional Forester?

8. Do you think that the ADVENT implementation is a priority issue with the Regional Forester?

9. If your forest developed a good program plan, but failed to use ADVENT, would the Regional Forester care?

10. Do you feel that those forests which use Advent to

a greater degree accrue any sort of organizational
benefit

   a) from the Regional Forester

   b) from the RO Staff

11. If one of your peers asked you to tell him/her
about ADVENT, how would you respond?

12. If one of your peers asked you to tell him/her
about Linear programming, how would you respond?

13. Have you ever worked on an ADVENT forest?

Key Personnel Questionaire

FOREST_____   date

NAME_____   position

1. Describe the FY 80 program plan development process.

2. Describe the FY 79 process by highlighting the differences from FY 80.

3. How would you compare FY 79 with FY 80 as far as:

    a. Quality

    b. Time required to build

    c. Other

4. Your opinion on the importance of the PPB process regarding

    a. Obtaining funds

    b. Other

5. Your opinion on the relative merits of
site-specific planning vs. unit-wide planning.

6. Your opinion on the increased use of technology
(computers) in program planning.

7. Impact of using ADVENT with site-specific projects:
    a. On man-hours

    b. On accuracy of program plan

c. Other impacts

8. How large of a change will site-specific ADVENT
implementation make to the following individual's
participation in the PPB process? Good or bad?
    a. District Rangers

    b. SO Resource Staff

    c. SO PPB Staff

    d. Forest Supervisor

    e. Anyone else

9. Would site-specific ADVENT implementation cause changes in the following areas? Good or bad?

   a. Organizational structure

   b. Decision making process

   c. Manning level

10. How serious a strain do you feel site specific ADVENT implementation would be on:

   a. Your manpower resources

   b. Your technical resources

11. How many times during the last six months has the

supervisor contacted you on*

   a. FY 80 program planning effort

   b. advent implementation

12. Do you think that the PPB process is a priority issue with the supervisor?

13. If your forest developed a good program plan, but failed to use ADVENT, would the supervisor care?

14. Do you feel that using ADVENT to a greater degree makes a forest "look good" to*

   a. The Regional Forester

   b. The RO Staff

15.   If one of your peers asked you what ADVENT is, how would you respond?

16.   If one of your peers asked you to tell him/her about linear programming, how would you respond?

17.   How long have you been connected with PPB?

18.   Have you worked on an ADVENT forest before?

REGION 6 FOREST RECEPTIVITY DATA

Variable*	1	2	3	4	5	6	7	8	9	10	11	12	13	14	15	16	17	18	19
1	4	5	3	4	4	4	2	2	2	3	4	5	4	2	2	4	4	4	1
2	3	5	3	1	3	4	3	3	5	2	4	4	4	3	3	3	4	4	4
3	3	4	3	2	5	2	1	5	4	4	3	5	5	2	3	4	4	1	1
4	4	4	2	2	4	4	3	4	5	5	2	3	5	2	2	3	5	2	4
5	4	5	5	4	5	1	3	3	5	5	2	5	2	1	4	3	5	1	1
6	4	4	5	3	4	3	1	4	5	4	2	4	5	2	4	3	5	1	2
7	2	2	3	2	2	1	1	2	4	4	1	3	2	1	1	4	3	1	2
8	3	2	3	2	2	2	2	1	2	4	1	2	2	1	1	4	2	1	2
9	2	5	5	2	5	2	1	3	5	4	1	4	3	1	3	4	4	2	2
10	3	4	4	2	4	2	3	4	4	5	2	3	4	2	2	2	4	2	3
11	2	5	1	3	2	2	5	5	2	4	1	3	5	2	5	3	5	5	3
12	2	5	2	1	2	4	4	3	3	3	1	4	3	3	4	2	3	4	3
13	2	5	2	2	2	2	5	1	3	3	1	1	3	3	4	4	4	5	1
14	3	5	5	1	5	2	1	4	5	5	1	4	3	1	3	2	4	5	3
15	5	5	5	3	4	3	5	3	5	5	2	3	5	3	2	2	4	5	1
16	2	5	5	1	1	1	5	2	5	5	1	4	2	1	1	1	4	5	3
17	5	3	5	1	4	3	5	2	5	5	2	1	5	1	1	3	4	5	3
18	2	3	2	2	5	1	1	4	4	5	1	1	1	1	2	1	5	2	1
19	2	4	3	1	5	2	2	5	4	5	2	2	2	2	2	2	5	1	1
20	2	2	2	2	5	1	1	4	4	5	1	2	1	1	2	1	4	1	1
21	2	2	3	1	4	2	2	4	4	5	2	2	2	2	2	2	5	2	2
22	2	2	2	2	4	2	1	2	2	5	2	5	2	2	2	2	2	2	2
23	2	3	2	2	3	2	1	2	2	5	2	2	5	2	2	2	3	2	2
24	5	5	5	3	5	2	2	4	2	4	2	4	3	2	2	3	3	1	1
25	4	5	3	1	4	1	3	1	4	3	1	4	3	1	1	1	2	1	1

*Variable descriptions are in Chapter 6, pp. 64-68.

The columns, numbered from 1 to 19 represent the nineteen administrative forests in Region 6. Thus, each column represents a particular forest's ratings on all 25 variables.

APPENDIX C

LETTERS FROM THE REGION 3 REGIONAL OFFICE

CONCERNING ADVENT IMPLEMENTATION

Date	Subject:
April 28, 1978	Initial Implementation--ADVENT
May 19, 1978	Implementation of ADVENT
May 22, 1978	National PD&B System (Note: addressed to the Chief of the Forest Service)
July 24, 1978	1981 Program Budget--ADVENT Process--Meeting July 10-11, 1978

UNITED STATES DEPARTMENT OF AGRICULTURE
FOREST SERVICE

R-3

REPLY TO: 1340 Management Improvement
(1900)

SUBJECT: Initial Implementation - ADVENT

April 28, 1978

TO: Forest Supervisors

The Gila, Kaibab and Lincoln National Forests have been selected as the first three units to be placed on the ADVENT computer process.

Computer Systems is developing technical information on equipment requirements including costs.

During the initial implementation stages, the Region will receive input from two Harvard University Research Assistants as part of a National contract. Details will be provided to the concerned units.

Periodic feedback will be provided to non-ADVENT units to keep them informed. Assuming the initial implementation is satisfactory, we will plan on adding about three more units to the ADVENT process next year.

M. J. Hassell

M. J. HASSELL
Regional Forester

cc: Deputy Regional Foresters
      Staff Unit Directors

UNITED STATES DEPARTMENT OF AGRICULTURE
FOREST SERVICE

Medlock

R-3

REPLY TO: 1930 Program Development and Budgeting   May 19, 1978

SUBJECT: Implementation of ADVENT

TO: Forest Supervisors, Gila, Kaibab,
and Lincoln National Forests

In our 1340 (1900) letter dated April 28, 1978, we stated that
your Forests had been selected for the ADVENT computer system.

Enclosed is the ADVENT Users Guide Manual.

To effectively and efficiently utilize the ADVENT process, it
is critical that we develop and implement a management strategy
and training effort. It is most important that you fully understand the process requires specific skills and full dedication
for successful implementation. One of the key factors for
technical applications is computer skills and ADP management
at the Forest level.

Currently we feel the following major tasks must be accomplished
by the target dates:

Task	Target Date
1. Forests and Regional Office establish and fill a Computer Specialist position, GS-9/11.	E.O.D. 7/30/78
2. Harvard University Research Assistant Lee Gremillion visits Forests and RO. The immediate objectives will be to assist us in developing our implementation strategy and training process.	Gila - 6/5, 6, 7/78 R.O. - 6/8 & 9/78 Lincoln - 6/12 & 13/78 Kaibab - 6/14 & 15/78
3. PP&B, Computer Systems, and Forest representatives visit the Stanislaus NF, Region 5, for ADVENT orientation (accompanied by R-5 PP&B Director, Bob Ground.)	5/30 & 31/78
4. Necessary Forest organization changes and responsibilities defined.	7/1/78
5. Computer hardware, including telecommunications, operational.	9/1/78

2
1930-Gila, et al. 5/19/78

Task	Target Date
6. General training sessions. One or two days per Forest.	7/17 - 21/78
7. Specific implementation training for all involved Forest personnel, including:	8/1 - 11/78 and as needed
a. Equipment b. FCCC - Job control language c. ADVENT system	
8. Forests develop projects and document on ADVENT project forms.	8/14 - 9/29/78
9. Forests input projects into computer. Project data edited and clean.	11/17/78
10. Forests develop alternative program strategies by aggregating projects in the ADVENT project data base. These will be various strategies to meet the 1981 Regional Direction.	11/17 - 12/15/78
11. Forest proposal available for Regional access.	1/5/79

M J Hassell

M. J. HASSELL
Regional Forester

Enclosure

cc: Medlock
     Coffelt
     Computer Systems

UNITED STATES DEPARTMENT OF AGRICULTURE
FOREST SERVICE

Medlock

R-3

REPLY TO: 1930 Program Development & Budgeting   May 22, 1978

SUBJECT: National PD&B System (Your ltr. of 4/5)

TO: Chief

Region Three plans to implement the modified ADVENT process on
three National Forests this year. A detailed schedule has been
developed and Forest commitment is very high. Also Mr. Gremillion
as part of the HBS Cooperative study is working with the Region
to help us implement ADVENT in the most effective manner. The
necessary justification of equipment upgrading and telecommuni-
cation is nearly complete. This should be available by June 1.

Early concurrence to proceed with modified ADVENT implementation
on three units would be appreciated.

GARY E. CARGILL
Acting Regional Forester

cc: Computer Systems
    Medlock
    Coffelt

UNITED STATES DEPARTMENT OF AGRICULTURE
FOREST SERVICE

R-3

REPLY TO: 1930 Program Development and Budgeting   July 24, 1978

SUBJECT: 1981 Program Budget--ADVENT Process--
Meeting July 10-11, 1978

TO: Forest Supervisors, Gila, Kaibab,
and Lincoln NFs

This letter documents the decisions that were reached in the
meeting of the Forest Supervisors of the three Forests selected
to implement the ADVENT process for FY 1981 program planning.
The purpose of the meeting was to obtain Forest Supervisor decisions to the implementation of key aspects available in the
ADVENT process.

The enclosed narrative contains a draft of the decisions that were
made by you. Please call Larry Medlock by July 31 to approve
or identify changes needed.

JOHN R. HAMMOND
Acting Director
Program Planning and Budget

Enclosure

DRAFT

I.   The Basic Forest Process

    A.   The issuance of direction and instructions to the District

        Rangers and Supervisors' staff (Ranger and staff participation).

        The direction and instructions package must contain the total

        information required by the Rangers and SO staff to prepare

        their program proposals.

        The package will identify the upper limits of the total subunit

        program beyond which the program is infeasible. This may

        include general instructions and definitions of optimum feasi-

        bility, maximum target ranges, maximum program activities,

        etc.

        The minimum essential level of targets and programs will be

        included. This minimum essential level will identify the

        targets and programs that may be further negotiated and those

        that must be planned and that are non-negotiable.

        In addition, the package will include all procedural instruc-.

        tions, forms, schedules, narrative reply requirements, etc.,

        necessary.

2·

B. <u>District Rangers and Supervisors' staff develop their programs.</u>
    During this phase of the Forest process, the District Rangers
    and Supervisors' staff prepare the total program for their sub-
    unit. The interaction of the Supervisor's Office and the Districts
    is most important. The SO staff will be available to assist
    Rangers in supplying information concerning standards, SO
    support for projects, completion of forms, etc.

C. <u>Validation of projects.</u> The validation of projects phase occurs
    when all subunits (Districts and SO) begin submitting their
    programs. This phase is a manual review of ADVENT form
    1930-1. The Supervisor's staff will review the District forms
    for program, coding, size of projects, and other instruction
    requirements.

D. <u>Input and validation reports.</u> This phase includes the computer
    input of the forms which will constitute a certain level of
    editing built into the program.

    Once the projects are in the system, a display of the submitted
    form will be immediately returned to the District Ranger for
    his projects and to Supervisor's staff for their projects.

When all projects are input for a subunit, selected reports will be developed and sent to the District Ranger and Supervisor's staff. These reports will be utilized to spot needed corrections, etc.

After this phase, the projects are accurate; thus, the decision-making process on a Forest level begins.

E. Decision-making and program development. During this phase, the Supervisor's staff utilizes the ADVENT computer capabilities to mix projects into various alternatives and develop recommended programs for the Forest.

At selected meetings, the staff will present alternative Forest programs to the Forest Supervisor and District Rangers. Thus, this phase results in the final Forest proposal to the Regional Forester.

This phase may require adjustment of projects for funding, skill requirements, standards, etc.

It is important to note that this process has three steps that require Ranger District and Supervisor's Office negotiation. These steps are A, B, and E.

4

II.   Project Descriptions

The ADVENT computer system is designed to combine various
entities of work and display feasible alternative programs.

These entities of work are termed projects. A project does not
necessarily conform to the definition of a project as we historically
know it, nor is it necessarily site specific. The only criteria for
the description of a project is to meet the decision-makers' requirement for evaluation, selection, allocation, and accountability.

To facilitate the decision-making process, it is imperative that
projects submitted be subjected to comparative analysis. They
must deal with as finite a subject matter as necessary to allow
full realization of decisions made.

The Forest Supervisors have jointly developed the following
descriptions of projects to be submitted:

Recreation Element

1.   Administration and operation of all developed sites
      except VIS.

2.   Administration and operation of all dispersed recreation areas.

3.   Administration and operation of all VIS sites.

4.   Administration and operation of all recreation trails.

5.   Maintenance of all developed sites except VIS.

6.   Maintenance of all dispersed recreation areas.

7.   Maintenance of all VIS sites.

8.   Maintenance of all recreation trails.

9.   Inventory, analysis, and plans for all developed recreation sites except VIS.

10. Inventory, analysis and plans for all dispersed recreation areas.

11. Inventory, analysis and plans for all VIS areas.

12. Inventory, analysis and plans for all recreation trails.

13. Rehabilitation (reconstruction) of each developed recreation site except VIS.

6

14. Rehabilitation (reconstruction) of each dispersed recreation facility.

15. Rehabilitation (reconstruction) of each VIS site.

16. Rehabilitation (reconstruction) of each recreation trail.

17. New construction of each developed recreation site except VIS.

18. New construction of each dispersed recreation facility.

19. New construction of each VIS site.

20. New construction of each recreation trail.

Note: Project descriptions 1 through 12 require District-wide projects, while projects 13 through 20 are site specific.

Wilderness Element

1. Administration and operation of wilderness trails (District-wide).

2. Administration and operation of wilderness areas (District-wide).

3. Maintenance of wilderness trails (District-wide).

4. Maintenance of wilderness facilities (District-wide).

5. Inventory, analysis and plans of wilderness trails (District-wide).

6. Inventory, analysis and plans of wilderness areas (District-wide).

7. Rehabilitation (reconstruction) of wilderness trails (each trail).

8. Rehabilitation (reconstruction) of wilderness facilities (each facility).

9. New construction of wilderness trails (each trail).

10. New construction of wilderness facilities (each facility).

Wildlife Element

1. Wildlife and fish surveys, plans and inventories, and cooperative relations (District-wide).

2. Threatened and endangered species surveys, plans, and inventories, and cooperative relations (District-wide).

8

3. Game, non-game, and fish habitat maintenance (District-wide).

4. Game, non-game, and fish habitat improvements (District-wide).

5. Threatened and endangered habitat maintenance (District-wide).

6. Threatened and endangered habitat improvement (District-wide).

Range Element

1. Operation, maintenance, and protection (District-wide).

2. Range improvement (by allotment).

Timber Element

1. Silvicultural examination and comprehensive examination (District-wide).

2. Saw timber and roundwood sale preparation (by sale).

3. Saw timber and roundwood sale administration (District-wide).

4.   Inventories and plans (District-wide).

5.   Tree improvement (District-wide).

6.   Reforestation - REF appropriation (District-wide).

7.   TSI - REF appropriation (District-wide).

8.   K-V (reforestation, TSI, etc.), BD, erosion control
     (District-wide).

9.   Miscellaneous sales, except roundwood, fuelwood, and
     sawlogs (District-wide).

10. Fuelwood, all (District-wide).

Water Element

1.   Operation, maintenance, and protection (District-wide).

2.   Watershed resource improvement (District-wide).

Minerals Element

1.   Geologic and mineral resources planning (District-wide).

2.   Management of mining activities (District-wide).

3.   Rehabilitation (District-wide).

10

Protection Element

1. Cooperative law enforcement (District-wide).

2. Cooperative search and rescue (District-wide).

3. Presuppression (District-wide).

4. Fuel maintenance (except BD) (District-wide).

5. Fuel capital investments (except BD) (District-wide).

6. Insect and disease control (District-wide).

7. Fire improvement construction, equipment, and structures (by project).

8. Planning (District-wide).

Soils Element

1. Operation, maintenance and protection (District-wide).

2. Capital investments (District-wide).

Lands Element

1. Lands administration (District-wide).

    a.   Land adjustment plans

    b.   Special studies

    c.   Land status

    d.   Land exchange (includes cash equalization)

    e.   Land line location and corner maintenance

2. Land line location, except support for other elements or projects (District-wide).

3. Special uses administration (District-wide).

4. Land management planning (includes RPA, Regional planning, and Forest planning) (District-wide).

5. Rights-of-way, excludes support for other elements or projects (includes L&WCF purchases and special purchases) (District-wide).

Facilities Element

1. Administration and planning (District-wide).

    a.   Transportation inventory and planning

    b.   Arterial and collector road maintenance

12

    c.   General purpose facilities maintenance (includes radios)

    d.   Dam inspection and maintenance

    e.   Trails

2.   Investments (by project).

    a.   General purpose construction

    b.   Arterial and collector roads construction and recon-
        struction (includes needed rights-of-way)

    c.   Bridges

    d.   Trails

    e.   Radio systems

Human and Community Development Element

1.   Planning for YCC, YACC, and other Human Resource Programs not tied to a project in another element (District-wide).

2.   Residence camps--all expenses that are not tied to a
project (District-wide).

3.   Construction of resident camps (by camp).

<u>General Management Element</u>

1.   Program management (District-wide).

2.   General administration (District-wide).

3.   Geometronics (District-wide).

III.   <u>Characteristics of Projects</u>

Projects developed must be self-sustaining and prioritized.   The
projects developed for each project description (see item II) will
be prioritized by identifying the minimum essential level for that
description as "1." The minimum essential level is defined as
the level below which the District or subunit cannot operate.   It
is important not to mix the minimum essential level with increased
needs.

In project descriptions where there is not a minimum essential
level, the first project for that category will be prioritized as "2."
For example, in the category of "new construction of wilderness
trails," it is not essential to construct a new trail for the District
to operate.

14

With this identification, the Forest Supervisor can readily identify each subunit minimum essential level as well as that of the Forest.

This item is strictly a Forest tool and must be supplemented to instruct how projects will be developed (by funding size, targets, program needs, etc.). This will enable various capabilities for mixing different projects to formulate programs.

IV.   Multi-Year Planning

A minimum requirement will be that each project description will contain 3-year levels (1981, 1982, 1983). Specific instructions for this item will be furnished by individual Forests.

V.   Skill Codes

The attached listing is the skill codes that will be used (exhibit I). Skill codes will not be required for general administration (GA).

VI.   Skill Costs

These costs will include salary, travel (except equipment use), and personal supplies necessary to enable an employee to effectively perform the duties.

15

VII.   Other Costs

Other costs will be identified in the following five categories:

    1.   Equipment FOR

    2.   Contracts

    3.   Supplies other than personal

    4.   Equipment use

    5.   Other

VIII. Personnel Ceiling Needs

Subunits will not use these work processes.

IX.   Program Management

The program management work process will be used as directed by the individual Forest Supervisor.

X.   Supervisor's Office Support for District Projects

District projects that require support from the Supervisor's Office will show that support directly on the District project. For example, the District timber sale project requiring SO engineering support will show the SO personnel on the District project. District

16

and SO coordination is of utmost importance in this concept. Subunits will not use the companion or alternative project concept.

Forest-wide crews that perform work on all Districts based on an approved plan will be planned on the SO subunit project (i.e., road maintenance). Each individual Forest will supplement this procedure.

1100 - SKILL CODES

ⴻXHIBIT 1

SKILL CODES		SKILL	DESCRIPTION
UNIT	OTHER UNIT		
101	201	Timber	Forester & Specialized Techs
102	202	Timber	Technicians & Aids
104	204	Engineering	Engineers & Specialized Techs
105	205	Engineering	Technicians & Aids
107	207	Fire Control	Foresters & Specialized Techs
108	208	Fire Control	Technicians & Aids
110	210	Recreation	Foresters & Specialized Techs
111	211	Recreation	Technicians & Aids
113	213	Landscape Arch.	Landscape Architect & Spec. Techs
114	214	Landscape Arch.	Technicians & Aids
115	215	Hydrology	Hydrologists & Specialized. Techs
116	216	Hydrology	Technicians & Aids
117	217	Soil Science	Soil Scientists & Spec. Techs
118	218	Soil Science	Technicians & Aids
119	219	Biology	Biologist & Specialized Techs
120	220	Biology	Technicians & Aids
121	221	Archaeology	Archaeologist & Spec. Techs
122	222	Archaeology	Technicians & Aids
123	223	Range Mgmt.	Range Conservationist & Spec.Techs
124	224	Range Mgmt.	Technicians & Aids
125	225	Geology	Geologist & Spec. Techs.
126	226	Geology	Technicians & Aids
127	227	Land Use Plng.	Professional Planners,Foresters,etc.
128	228	Land Use Plng.	Technicians & Aids in LUP
130	230	Genetics	Geneticist
131	231	Economics	Economists, Management Analysts
132	232	Social Science	Sociologists, Educators
133	233	Social Science	Technicians & Aids

-11.1-

1100 - SKILL CODES (cont'd)

SKILL CODES		SKILL	DESCRIPTION
UNIT	OTHER UNIT		
134	234	Public Inform	Forester, PIO's, Naturalists, Historian & Specialized Techs.
135	235	Public Inform	Technicians, Aids, Receptionists, Caretakers
137	237	Lands	Forester, Appraisers & Realty Spec
139	239	Right-of-Way	Forester, Right-of-Way Spec.
141	241	Mineral Examin.	Mining Engineers
143	243	YCC Program	YCC Director & Specialized Staff
144	244	YCC Program	YCC Technicians & Aids
145	245	Comp Operations	Computer Spec. & Analyst
146	246	Comp Operations	Computer Progr. & Operator
148	248	Law Enforcement	Law Enforcement Specialist
50	250	Pilot	Airplane Pilot
152	252	Scaling	Scalers
153	253	Mechanics	Automotive & Heavy Equip. Mech.
155	255	Equip. Operator	Equipment Operator
157	257	Skilled Labor	Carpenters, Plumber, Cement Finisher, Cooks, etc.
158	258	General Labor	Laborers (Wage Grade)
160	260	Radio Tech.	Electronics Technician
161	261	Radio Tech.	Technician, Aids - Radio
178	278	Older American	Older American Enrollee
179	279	YCC	YCC Enrollee
180	280	NYC, etc.	Special Manpower Programs
181	281	Ecology Corps.	California State
182	282	F.S. Volunteers	N.F. Volunteer Program

-11.2-

1100 - SKILL CODES (cont'd)

SKILL CODES		SKILL	DESCRIPTION
UNIT	OTHER UNIT		
183	283	Other Volunteers	Boy Scouts, 4 WD, Audubon, etc.
184	284	Timber Oper. Coop	Timber Purchaser Work
185	285	Other Coop.	Permittee Coop. Work
186	286	Contributed F.S.	Fire, Doing Recreation Work, etc.
190	290	Clerical	Clerks
193	293	Bus. Management	AO, AA, Adm. Tech., Pers. Off., Contract Spec., B&F, Resource AA, etc.
198	298	Program Mgmt.	Supervisor's and Ranger's staff
199	299	Line Management	Forest Supervisor, Deputy FS, Rangers

-11.3-

APPENDIX D

FOREST PROGRAM PLANNING DOCUMENTS

1. Gila National Forest letter of September 11, 1978:
    1981 Program Planning Procedures and Direction Package

2. Lincoln National Forest: Direction Package distributed
    at Ranger/Staff meeting, August 10, 1978.

UNITED STATES DEPARTMENT OF AGRICULTURE
FOREST SERVICE

GILA NF

REPLY TO: 1930 Program Development   September 11, 1978

SUBJECT: FY 1981 Forest Direction

TO: All District Rangers & SO Staff

Enclosed is the 1981 Forest Direction consisting of the following sections:

I. Direction

    A. Mimimum essential program
    B. Maximum program
    C. List of projects by work activity/work type for FY 81

II. Procedural Instructions

    A. Forms
    B. Support
    C. Skill Codes
    D. Schedules
    E. Listing of appropriations and functions (See Exhibit III)

A. Minimum Essential Program
    (Base Forest Program)

The following shifts (increases & decreases) from our 79 Base Program or Program Areas were agreed to at our Ranger/Staff Meeting on 8/21/78

    1. Increases

        a. Purchaser Credit Road - Cost will be in our minimum level. To remove the timber in FY 81, we will not reduce quality of roads.

        b. I.D. Team involvement in Land Management Planning.

        c. Fuelwood - Sales and Administration. This is to be accomplished by multi-financing where feasible.

        d. Increase in Engineering Design for Purchaser Credit Roads. The increase in miles of P.C. roads for 1982 & 83 sales requires this increase.

        e. Increase in R/W Appraisal and Purchase.

2. Decreases

    a. Reduce Coop Law in Catron & Sierra Counties.

    b. Special Uses - TG&E.

    c. Site prep for natural regeneration.

    d. 50% of reforestation targets.

    e. Range Revegetation - Only projects will be those involving invasion, remainder of revegetation is to be accomplished through fuelwood program.

    f. Pre-Suppression - reduce 16%.

    g. Eliminate Wildlife Improvement Construction.

    h. VIS - Only Gila Center will be involved.

    i. Recreation Development Sites - Dipping Vat & Mimbres Campgrounds only areas to be operated at full service level, rest to be operated at reduced service level.

3. Targets

The targets for the minimum program are the same as those for our minimum 79 program with the exceptions of the shifts for the 1981 program listed under increases and decreases.

B. Maximum Program

No projects are to be proposed, if they are not reasonable nor feasible to attain (no pie-in-the-sky projects).

Projects above the minimum level are to be submitted by priority.

First priorities above base are those programs or projects reduced or deleted from the minimum essential program.

In order to enable us to analyze and make decisions on a forest program, all elements except the Range Element will be held to a maximum of 10 priorities (priority 1 thru 10). In the Range element we have the capability to go to 99 (ninety-nine). This is necessitated by programming by allotments for improvements.

C. List of Projects by Work Activity and Work Type

Following is a list of projects by work, activity and work types, see Exhibit I. This list is not to be added to. As you will note, this list differs from the list of projects we disseminated in August. This resulted from the new MIH and amendments to the MIH, which were not available when the three forests under ADVENT met in early July.

3
1930-Rangers & Staff-9/11/78

You will note that most codes are held to alpha-numeric. One
basic concept we must keep in mind.is to keep the process as simple
as possible. The more codes we use, the more data we generate,
which compounds any analysis and decision making process. Also
unless we recognize a need for going beyond Alpha Codes for decision
making, we do not need to create nice-to-have-data.

II. Procedural Instructions

A. Forms

    1. Use 6500-154s and 155s. These documents are invaluable in the
    planning process and also for new employees at allocation time.

    2. Form 1930-1. Data Document Form

        a. Utilize the back of this form as a 1900-4 except for salaries,
        per diem and equipment use.

        Also narratives for increments above base.

        b. Narratives

        .All increments will have narratives. These are to be on an
        individual form for that proposal. Narratives are to consist
        of a brief statement on the environmental & social consequences
        of the project.

    3. Instructions for completing Form 1930-1

    Block A.
    Sub Unit Name - Enter name of Sub Unit.
    Companion/Alternative Project Exists - No entry.
    Sheet No. _____ of _____. Complete regardless of whether more than one
    form is used.
    Date - Enter 1978.

    Block B.
    Sub Unit - Enter sub-unit number.
    Project - This is where we code priority of projects. Cross out
    project and write in priority. Make no entry for minimum level.
    Priorities are within elements. For example, the Timber and
    Recreation Elements can both have a priority 1 thru 10. You are
    to prioritize projects within elements.

    Increment - This is the Element Code Block. Enter the element codes
    in MIH. Example, Timber Element, enter "E".

    Program Area - Enter Project Number from Project Codes. Example:
    Recreation Trail Mtce. enter 9. This entry is in 3rd space. Should
    project number be 2 digits, entry will be 2nd and 3rd spaces.

4
1930–Rangers/Staff–9/11/78

Region Station Area – Enter 03.
Planning Area – No entry.
Forest or Unit – Enter 06.
District – No entry.
State – Enter 035.
County – Enter County Code Numbers for County.
          Project proposed in:
          Grant – 017
          Catron – 003
          Sierra – 051
          Hidalgo – 023
Congressional District – No entry.
Funding Class – Enter "1" in third space for minimum program.
          Enter "2" in third space for above minimum.

In project descriptions where there is not a minimum essential level, the first project for that category in funding class is "2", with a priority assigned within that element. An example would be construction of a new trail. It is not essential to construct a new trail for the sub unit to operate.

Eco Region, Analysis Group & Ranking – No entry. We do not have these available at this time.

Block C.
Card Type 1 – Enter 1981 Program.
Project Name – Enter project name from Exhibit I.
Brief Description – Be concise, limit to 4 words or less.
Prepared By, Approved By, & Date – No entry.

Block D.
Enter the appropriate output description, unit of measure, output code, and element code from the Management Information Handbook. (Do not code effects)

Block E. – Do not use decimals.

Block F. – No entry.

Block G. – No explanation necessary, utilize same process as FY 80 Program, but use new MIH (8/4/78).

Block H. – Dollar cost will be entered to the nearest whole dollar. Do not show decimals.

4. Multi-Year Planning

Each project description will contain 3 year levels (1981, 82, & 83).

5
1930-Rangers & Staff-9/11/78

B. <u>Support</u>

An acitivity may be included in any element as a support activity for
the production of outputs. This principle should insure that all
resource coordination funding needs have been recognized and displayed
in proposals.

In determining support activities, the following principle is useful:

Support during the environmental analysis, including inventory,
analysis, and prescription development phases of a project <u>will be
funded from the function providing the support.</u>

There is one exception to the above, that being engineering support <u>not
involving transportation planning, roads, trails (FR&T) etc.</u> All other
engineering support is funded by the function originating the project.

To illustrate the support concept, the following chart displays phases
of a project and funding responsibilities for each phase.

Project Phases	Primary Function Orig Proj	Support Resource Coordination Input					
1. Project identification	031	080	091	071	178	116	130
2. Inventory & EAR Prep & ID Review	X	X	X	X	X	X	X
3. EAR Review	X	X	X	X	X	X	X
4 Doing Project	X						

C. <u>Skill Codes</u>

1. The attached listing is the skill codes that will be used (Exhibit II).
   Skill Codes are not required for G.A. We have also tied functions to
   the skills to assist in exhibiting support.

   *The following basic principle applies to Skill Codes:

   100 Series - Skill is available on Sub Unit.

   200 Series - Skill Code not available on Sub Unit.

   *Do not try to compound, keep simple.

2. <u>Skill Costs</u> - Skill Costs, salary, travel (except heavy equipment use),
   and personal supplies necessary to enable an employee to effectively
   perform the duties have been figured by this office and will be
   entered into the computer, therefore eliminating the hand methods of
   calculation.

6
1930-Rangers & Staff-9/11/78

3. Other Costs - Other costs will be indentified in the following
   categories and by code:

Code	Costs
1	Equipment For
2	Contracts
3	Supplies other than personal
4	Heavy Equipment Use
5	Other

D. Schedules

   1. District & SO Staff submission of programs - October 20, 1978.

   2. Validation of projects & programs by SO Staff & Computer Specialist.

   3. Decision making & forest program - 11/30/78.

Planning Procedures for Human Resource Programs

This direction for Human Resource Programs differs from previous direction.

All Human Resource Programs will be planned in element H, "Human and
Community Development". The work units produced by the Human Resource
Programs will also be shown in element H. The work units reflected must be
unduplicated in other elements. If there are work units that the Human
Resources programs are contributing a higher standard toward (such as
Recreation Developed Site Reduced Service), then there would be no work
units planned but the funding would be planned in the activity on which
they are working (such as A13 Developed Recreation Sites, Reduced Service
Management).

These projects will use the proper work activity code to reflect the work
being done. For example, work activity code E04 with YCC appropriation 029
in element H would identify the YCC funds and the reforestation work done by
Youth Conservation Corps employees. If reforestation funds are needed to
supplement the project, they will be identified by the work activity code
E04, reforestation appropriation 006, function 033, and element code H.

In the Human Resources program two types of primary outputs will be measured;
(1) dollar value of work completed, and (2) number of hours, weeks, or years
of participation by program enrollees. In addition, if the Human Resources
program produces a primary output of another element, the output will be
shown.

Outputs must not be duplicated in other elements.

This procedure will consolidate all Human and Community Development dollars
and supplementing dollars in the Human and Community Development Element.

7
1930-Rangers & Staff-9/11/78

Chuck Jourden will be visiting field units the following dates to check
on progress and assist with major problems:

9/22	Silver City
9/26	Luna
9/27	Quemado & Reserve
9/28	Glenwood
10/3	Beaverhead
10/4	T or C
10/5	Mimbres
10/6	Wilderness

ROBERT M. WILLIAMSON
Forest Supervisor

Enclosures

RMW/fh

LINCOLN NATIONAL FOREST: distributed August 10, 1978.

A.   RECREATION

Operate and maintain all developed public facilities at FSL.

D-1	177,110 PAOT Days
D-2	424,355
D-3	41,975
D-4	10,950

The above targets include observation sites and VIS sites.

Manage recreation special use permits at FSL.

Trail maintenance: 75 percent of district miles to Level I, 15 percent to Level II, and 10 percent to Level III.

Maintain and enforce ORV closures according to implementation plan.

Prepare feasibility studies for trail head facilities at Argentina Canyon, Wilderness Ridge, and Elder Canyon.

Complete feasibility studies for at least one identified site on each district.

Emphasize cave management including VIS, signing and protection.

Continue host role program training and implementation.

Obtain cultural resource clearance on all ground disturbing projects as part of project costs.

Conduct visual resource analysis on all products that effect the landscape as part of project costs.

Maintain dispersed recreation facilities and manage dispersed recreation to high quality standards.

Objectives for increased recreation funding:

    Construct Dog Canyon Trail.

    Heavy maintenance on developed facilities that does not include major facility reconstruction over $25,000.

    Trail maintenance to level specified in trail inventory.

    Survey and design remainder of Rim Trail (Cloudcroft RD).

    Complete dispersed recreation plan on each district.

    Survey and design of Last Chance Campground.

Increase management level of dispersed recreation and cave management.

Develop dispersed recreation information for:

Wildlife	D-1, D-2 and D-4, and D-3
Plants	D-1, D-2 and D-4 combined, and D-3
Birds	D-1, D-2 and D-4, and D-3
Trail Maps	D-1, D-2, and D-3

Provide for host role program coordination and VIS person on each district.

B. WILDERNESS

Manage White Mountain and Guadalupe Wildernesses to protect resources and to be good FS "hosts."

Prepare Wilderness Management plan for the Guadalupe.

Trail maintenance to Level I on all trails and to Level II on the heaviest used trails.

Provide a wilderness ranger for the period from May 15 to September 15 in White Mountain Wilderness.

Direction for increased funding:

Maintain trails to level prescribed in the trail inventory.

Remove non-conforming structures in White Mountain and Guadalupe Wildernesses.

Extend wilderness ranger in White Mountain to include fall hunting season.

C. WILDLIFE AND FISH

Conduct at least 24 browse utilization surveys on key areas delineated by both the Forest Service and the New Mexico Game Department.

Provide technical assistance and cooperate with the Game Department in developing wildlife programs on the District.

Provide maintenance on wildlife waters.

Provide maintenance on two wildlife trick tanks per district.

Provide maintenance on at least one wildlife enclosure per district.

Mark and protect at least two snag trees per acre on all fuelwood sales scheduled for FY-81. Mark and protect any turkey roost trees or raptor nests found in these areas.

Objectives for increased funding:

Smokey Bear District

Maintain at least two miles of stream channel.

Develop a stream management plan for one of the district streams.

Prune 50 acres of browse in the Capitans.

Develop two - five-acre wildlife enclosures with drinkers.

Cloudcroft District

Develop a prescribed burning plan for the west side of the Sacramentos and burn at least 50 acres of the mountain brush type.

Guadalupe District

Maintain Peregrine Falcon habitat. This will probably involve some type of habitat manipulation which will in turn maintain a particular prey species.

Mayhill District

Develop one - five-acre wildlife enclosure with a permanent water source located in the confines of the enclosure.

Conduct a riparian survey and develop a fencing plan for the riparian areas on the district.

General - Forest-wide to the Extent Feasible

Extend pipelines from livestock waters to a wildlife drinker in an adjacent protected area (heavy brush - PJ timber, etc.) and surround this drinker with a five-acre enclosure.

Provide escape and access ramps on all livestock waters developed in FY-81 and on 20 percent of the remaining livestock waters.

Prescribe burn additional acres of the mountain brush type on the west side of the Sacramentos.

Prescribe burn areas of mountain and/or desert shrub in the Guadalupes based on the District Fire Plan developed in FY-78 and 79.

Prune additional acres of browse in the Capitans.

Construct wildlife trick tanks on the Mayhill, Smokey Bear, and Cloudcroft Districts. Locate these waters within a five-acre fenced enclosure.

Develop one seep or spring on the Smokey Bear and Cloudcroft Districts. Surround these developments with a five-acre enclosure.

Fence feasible portions of the riparian zone on the Mayhill District and Cloudcroft District. Plant these areas with broad leaf shrubs and trees.

Protect existing snags (wildlife tree signs) and generate new snags (by girdling) on old timber and/or fuelwood sales where public firewood cutting is still permissible or uncontrolled.

Bird house construction and distribution for cavity nesting species in the PJ/grassland types on the Smokey Bear and Guadalupe Districts.

Create five-acre openings in the PJ type on the Guadalupe and Smokey Bear Districts in conjunction with woodland management plans.

C. WILDLIFE AND FISH

Conduct at least 24 browse utilization surveys on key areas delineated by both the Forest Service and the New Mexico Game Department.

Provide technical assistance and cooperate with the Game Department in developing wildlife programs on the District.

Provide maintenance on wildlife waters.

Provide maintenance on two wildlife trick tanks per district.

Provide maintenance on at least one wildlife enclosure per district.

Mark and protect at least two snag trees per acre on all fuelwood sales scheduled for FY-81. Mark and protect any turkey roost trees or raptor nests found in these areas.

Objectives for increased funding:

Smokey Bear District

Maintain at least two miles of stream channel.

Develop a stream management plan for one of the district streams.

Prune 50 acres of browse in the Capitans.

Develop two - five-acre wildlife enclosures with drinkers.

Cloudcroft District

Develop a prescribed burning plan for the west side of the Sacramentos and burn at least 50 acres of the mountain brush type.

Guadalupe District

Maintain Peregine Falcon habitat. This will probably involve some type of habitat manipulation which will in turn maintain a particular prey species.

Mayhill District

Develop one - five-acre wildlife enclosure with a permanent water source located in the confines of the enclosure.

Conduct a riparian survey and develop a fencing plan for the riparian areas on the district.

General - Forest-wide to the Extent Feasible

D.   RANGE

Range Administration (051)

Range Allotment Analysis Program D01

Cloudcroft and Mayhill Ranger Districts in planning for FY-81 will
submit for review and/or approval a long-term (5-year) Allotment
Analysis Program. The program will consider priority needs by fiscal
year for allotments which need attention to either bring stocking in
line with capacity or for data needed to develop proper management
and associated improvement needs. Consistency in planning from one
fiscal year to another, along with quality of work performance, is
essential to accomplish the needs outlined in the conceptual plan
for the Sacramento Mountains. As a minimum, each district should
program two Range Allotment Analyses for the fiscal year.

Guadalupe Ranger District submit for review and/or approval a 5-year
plan outlining a Range Allotment Analysis Program. The program should
take into consideration the time frames necessary to fully document
the range, wildlife and soils resource inventory needs on problem
allotments where reduction in numbers are anticipated to obtain proper
grazing management. As a minimum, one (1) Range Allotment Analysis or
reanalysis should be programmed for FY-81.

Smokey Bear Ranger District submit for review and/or approval a 5-year
Range Allotment Analysis Program. Priority for allotment analysis
work to be performed will consider stocking adjustments and management
needs including range improvements. A minimum of two Range Analyses
should be planned for FY-81.

Development of the above noted Allotment Analysis Program should include,
in addition to studies needed for reducing numbers, studies on allotment
where increases are anticipated or deserving.

Production/Utilization Studies D02

All districts submit a listing of those allotments on which they plan
to complete production/utilization studies. Priority for studies should
be based on those allotments where validation of capacity is needed, a
new management plan is being developed or a major range improvement
program is programmed. As a minimum, each district should plan on
performing P/u studies on two (2) allotments.

Allotment Management Plans & Permittee Plans D01

In cooperation with permittes, each district should, as a minimum,
obtain signed management plans on two grazing allotments.

Since many of our grazing permittees are now operating without any
agreed upon management direction, an effort must be put forth to obtain,

as a minimum, annual permittee plans by which allotments will be
managed. Each district should strive to get annual plans on all
allotments where formal plans are not in existence.

Range Inspections (051) D02

A minimum of 35 percent of the allotments on each district will be
inspected and a report documenting the inspection filed. Each district
should submit a proposed inspection schedule for FY-81.

Improvements (053)

Structural Improvements D05

Each district should develop a program of structural improvement needs
for FY-81. The program will consider priorities established in the
Allotment Analysis Program as well as existing obligations associated
with existing or anticipated management plans that will be in effect
by FY-81. Funding level will most likely be similar to those now in
existence and thus, planning should be accomplished with this in mind.

Non-Structural Improvements D04

Each district should submit non-structural projects that are now in
their program or those anticipated by FY-81. Programs for consideration
should be those on allotments where stocking and management is at a level
that will protect the investment cost of such proposals.

Maintenance of Structural Improvements D06

Each district should submit maintenance project proposals that they feel
are necessary to prevent a loss in an existing major investment. Maintenance projects should not be those normally performed by grazing permittees.

Range Betterment Funds D05

Each district should submit anticipated funding requests for the use
of Range Betterment Funds. In programming the request for the funds,
you must consider that the allotment on which the funds are to be
utilized must be capable of supporting the grazing obligation and must
be operating under an approved management plan.

E.   TIMBER

Administer all contracts to acceptable level of quality.

Prepare and sell firewood program in convenient areas at 20 MM level.
Combine free use in selected areas for clean-up only.

Accomplish compartment examination work at maintenance level in existing
plantations.

Complete minimum sale preparation work necessary for 5.00 MM sell in FY's 82-83.

Complete reforestation of 800 a͟c͟r͟e͟s including backlog and current.

Objectives for increased funding:

Plant A͟D͟D͟I͟T͟I͟O͟N͟A͟L͟ 2͟0͟0͟ ~~minimum of 1,000~~ acreas forest-wide. Add increments up to feasible performance level. Plan support work for FY-82.

Use only qualified and properly trained and supervised people in all phases of sale preparations and administration.

Continue free use firewood program as a means of reducing debris accumulation at about the same level as FY-79. Increase by increment to maximum feasible program.

Complete 16,000 acres of compartment examination, TSI and Reforestation 10,000 Cloudcroft RD, and 6 m Mayhill RD.

Prepare and sell 7.3 mmbf in Apache, Cloudcroft RD, and Hugues Seep, Mayhill RD, sales.

Compute work to be done in 1981 that is necessary to meet 82-85 sales.

Conduct Forest Free-improvement Program (SO).

Sell 500 M in salvage sales as a separate program from regulated sell.

F.   WATERSHED MANAGEMENT

Each district should, as a minimum, submit for review a watershed project proposal for FY-81. The proposal should be one that requires new restoration work or one where maintenance needs are critical from a resource protection need.

In view of the U.S. Supreme Court decision concerning the Mimbres Case, each district should consider the possible need to file applications for water needs. Each district should plan to initiate four (4) cases.

Support demands f͟o͟r͟ ~~from~~ the hydrologist for all resource activities must be identified in the projects by skill codes.

G.   MINERALS

Complete hazardous mine inventory.

Continue program of validity determinations on those claims where unauthorized structures are located (Smokey Bear RD). Complete two cases.

Projects for increased funding:

Submit proposals to eliminate hazardous mine situations.

H.   HUMAN AND COMMUNITY DEVELOPMENT

Completely integrate human resource programs into the regular Forest Service programs.

Utilize manpower programs to the maximum extent possible.

Conduct 75 percent intensive safety inspection of facilities. Shut down any facility with a class A or B hazard which cannot be corrected.

Conduct walk-through safety inspection of 25 percent of facilities.

Inspect a cross section of work projects to insure safe and healthful working conditions and procedures.

Inspect each manpower program during first two weeks of operation.

Inspect project fires daily.

Targets Minimum Level

YCC

D-1	600 person days	(15 enrollees)
D-2	1200 person days	(30 enrollees)

YACC

Engineering	2900 person days	(15 enrollees)

Work to be coordinated with individual ranger districts by Engineering.

Senior Community Service Employment

D-1	2400 hours	(2 enrollees)
D-3	1200 hours	(1 enrollee)
SO	3600 hours	(3 enrollees)

CETA

D-3	600 person days	(15 enrollees)
SO	80 person days	(2 enrollees)

Volunteers In The National Forests

D-1   (1 enrollee)
D-2   (2 enrollees)

Districts will need to compute how many person days of work are needed. These enrollees are primarily for your Recreation Host Program. All districts are encouraged to actively seek out and define those tasks a volunteer can accomplish.

J.   LANDS

Continue land purchase actions in Bonito Campsite as scheduled in RAC.

Start purchase negotiations in Nogal-Tortolita and Cloudcroft ~~Campsites~~ *composites* if these campsites have been approved by 1981.

Continue land exchanges in progress:

D-1	Canning	40 acres selected
D-2	Mills	180 acres selected
D-4	One case	

Initiate or accept only high-priority new cases. Include appraisal costs in funding needs.

Manage and inspect special uses according to manual frequency.

D-1	106
D-2	88
D-3	18
D-4	42

Review all special use permits indicated in Forest Supplement for 1981.

Respond to all special use applications in a timely manner.

Title claims and occupancy cases:

D-1	2
D-2	2
D-4	2

Administer and coordinate interagency agreements with military, NSF, and other government agencies. Update and prepare new ones as needed.

R/O/W requisition as indicated in the 5-year R/O/W plan. Appraisal costs are to be included in funding needs. Estimate $2,000 per case for contract appraisal. Indicate priority for each R/O/W by district.

		Survey	Acquisition
D-2	Cloud Country West (2 roads)		X (Otero County)
D-1	Elder Canyon or Water Canyon	X	
D-1	Eagle Lake		X
D-1	Bernardo Gap		X (Lincoln County)
D-2	Old Railroad Grade-osha Trail		X
D-1	Maverick Canyon	X	
D-4	Jim Lewis Canyon	X	

Projects for increased funding:

    Initiate and accept additional land exchange proposals..

    Additional R/O/W cases for survey by priority.

    Accelerate RAC purchase program for all ~~campsites.~~ *COMPOSITES*

    Revise Forest and District L.O.A.P.

    Resolve new occupancy trespass and title claims as a result of increased LLL.

Land Line Location J06

Land line location and posting should be planned with each appropriate project.

Miles of Posted Boundary 063

Backlog location and posting should be programmed in lands element.

Miles of Boundary Maintained J07

Land line boundary and corner maintenance should be planned for each district. Based upon a 10-year maintenance cycle, 10 percent of each district posted boundaries should be maintained each year.

District	Total Miles of Boundary to be Posted	Miles of Boundary Posted to Standard as of 10/1/78	Projected by FY-81
1	695.5	22.50	88.
2	344.25	94.00	144.
3	221.25	47.50	70.
4	474.50	117.00	153.
Total	1,735.50	281.00	455.

K.   SOILS

Projected soil scientist demands for each district are needed. Identify in skill codes. Probable needs for soil scientist and hydrologist inputs will be in the following areas:

    Watershed Projects - All revegetation projects and other large watershed projects.

    <u>Range Allotment Analyses</u> - Particularly allotments that may be
reduced and other problem allotments.

    <u>Timber Sales</u>

    <u>Reforestation Projects</u>

    <u>Recreation and Lands</u> - Assistance in location and planning of
campgrounds and facilities, for example.

    <u>Miscellaneous Management Services</u> - Mining, claims, other special
use permits, training, etc.

L.   FACILITIES ELEMENT

Maintenance of all facilities, fire and general purpose structures,
roads, radios, dams, etc., should be provided to quality standard.
Engineering will assist in preparing districts' programs.

Maintain both transportation system and travelway inventories.

Full operation of Forest road maintenance management system.

Provide traffic surveillance to provide credible management data on
traffic volumes and classification on all roads in maintenance levels
III, IV, and V.

Schedule inspection and maintenance to a full service level on 100
percent cf all roads in maintenance level IV and V. (See FSM 7709.15--
12.24 7 25.)

Schedule inspection and maintenance to a full service level on 50 percent
of all roads in maintenance level III.

Schedule inspection and maintenance to a full service level on at least
25 percent of all roads in maintenance level II.

Schedule inspection and maintenance of all roads in maintenance level I,
together with installation and maintenance of all required closure
devices and signing.

Schedule inspection and maintenance of all buildings and facilities,
correct all health and safety deficiencies, maintain facility to prevent
degrading of structure.

Schedule feasibility studies for all capital investments over $25,000
for construction in FY-84 and beyond.

Perform inspection on all dams on FS land in conformance with FSM 7500 and the Dam Safety Act. Review and revise current operation and maintenance plans as necessary.

Perform annual condition surveys on all water and sanitation facilities not routinely maintained as outlined in FSM 7400.

Schedule upgrading and/or reconstruction of water systems not in compliance with the Safe Drinking Water Regulation.

N.   GENERAL ADMINISTRATION

Develop general administration budgets by subunit.

Develop plans for training and career development as mandated by either the Forest Service or CSC. (Red card quals, basic supervision, sale administration, etc.).

Meet Regional and Forest goals for EEO and Civil Rights - develop costs and plans for upward mobility, Affirmative Action, recruitment, and Civil Rights training.

P.   PROTECTION

Maintain fire organization positions of: District FMO's, Supervisory Prevention Techniques and Forest Dispatcher. Hold support and facilitating services at 80 percent of FY-78 level.

Implement remainder of fire organization at FY-78 level during established fire season only.

Keep slash reduction current.

Complete maintenance on 10 percent of constructed fuel breaks.

Maintain law enforcement agreements at current level.

Objectives for increased funding:

    Bring protection forces, support and facilitating services up to FY-78 level.

Accomplish at a minimum:

Prescribe Burn	750 acres
Fuel Reduction	500 acres
Fuel Break Construction	100 acres
Backlog Slash Treatment	500 acres

Complete preliminary work on data needed for FOCUS RUN in 1982, based on Forest Land Management plan draft. (Forest Dispatcher)

Increase cooperative law enforcement contracts as needed.

Forest-wide inventory of mistletoe problem.

References

Allan, Harvey. "Factors Making for Implementation Success and Failure." *Management Science* 16:6.

Anthony, Robert N. *Planning and Control Systems: A Framework for Analysis.* Boston: Graduate School of Business Administration, Harvard University, 1965.

Bass, Bernard M. and Vaughan, James A. *Training in Industry: The Management of Learning.* Belmont, California: Wadsworth Publishing Company, 1966.

Benjamin, Robert I. *Control of the Information System Development Life Cycle.* New York: Wiley, 1971.

Blumenthal, Sherman C. *Management Information Systems: A Framework for Planning and Development.* Englewood Cliffs: Prentice-Hall, 1969.

Brandon, Dick H. *Management Standards for Data Processing.* New York: Van Nostrand, 1963.

Burch, John G. and Strater, Felix. *Information Systems: Theory and Practice.* Santa Barbara, California: Hamilton Publishing, 1974.

Burke, W. Warner. *Current Issues and Strategies in Organization Development.* New York: Human Science Press, 1977.

Bylinsky, Gene. "Here Comes the Second Computer Revolution." *Fortune* (November 1975): 138.

Cale, Edward G. "Implementing Standard Computer-Based Systems in Decentralized Organizations." Unpublished doctoral thesis, Graduate School of Business Administration, Harvard University, 1979.

Campbell, Donald T. and Stanley, Julian C. *Experimental and Quasi-Experimental Designs for Research.* Chicago: Rand-McNally, 1963.

Canning, R. "In Your Future: Distributed Systems?" *EDP Analyzer.* August, 1973.

Carder, D. Ross. *Unified Planning and Decision Making.* U. S. Forest Service, 1973.

Chin, Robert and Benne, Kenneth D. "General Strategies for Effecting Changes in Human Systems." In *The Planning of Change.* Bennis, Warren G. *et al.* (eds.). New York: Holt, Rinehart and Winston, 1976, pp. 22–54.

Clark, Peter A. *Action Research and Organizational Change.* London: Harper & Row, 1972.

Clifton, H. D. *Systems Analysis for Business Data Processing.* New York: Petrocelli Books, 1974.

Cougar, J. Daniel and Knapp, Robert W. *Systems Analysis Techniques.* New York: Wiley, 1974.

Cummings, T. G. "Sociotechnical Systems: An Intervention Strategy." In *Current Issues and Strategies in Organizational Development.* New York: Human Sciences Press, 1977.

Dalton, Gene W.; Lawrence, Paul R.; and Greiner, Larry E. *Organizational Change and Development.* Homewood: Irwin, 1970.

Datapro. "EDP Cost Reduction and Control." *EDP Solutions.* Deltran, N.J.: Datapro Research Corporation, 1978, p. E40-300-414.

———. "Logical Machine Corporation ADAM." *Datapro Reports on Minicomputers.* Deltran, N.J.: Datapro Research Corporation, 1976, p. M11-587-101.

Davis, Gordon B. *Management Information Systems: Conceptual Foundations, Structure, and Development.* New York: McGraw Hill, 1974.

Denova, Charles. *Establishing a Training Function.* Englewood Cliffs: Educational Technology Publications, 1971.

Dickson, Gary W. and Powers, Richard F. "MIS Project Management: Myths, Opinions and Reality." University of Minnesota, Management Information Systems Research Center, 1971.

Forrester, Jay W. *Industrial Dynamics.* Cambridge: MIT Press, 1961.

Ginzberg, Michael J. "A Detailed Look at Implementation Research." Massachusetts Institute of Technology, Center for Information Systems Research, 1974, Report CISR-4.

Gremillion, Lee. "USFS Region 6 ADVENT Implementation: Summary Report of the USFS/HBS Cooperative Study Team." Graduate School of Business Administration, Harvard University, 1978.

Gross, Neal; Giaquinta, Joseph B.; and Bernstein, Marilyn. *Implementing Organizational Innovations: A Sociological Analysis of Planned Educational Change.* New York: Basic Books, 1971.

Henson, Joe. "Technology." *Datamation* 23:10 (October 1977): 172.

Huysmans, Jan H. *The Implementation of Operations Research.* New York: Wiley, 1970.

Ives, Blake; Hamilton, Scott; and Davis, Gordon B. "A Framework for Research in Computer-Based Management Information Systems." Minneapolis: Management Information Systems Research Center, University of Minnesota, 1977, MISRC-WP-77-01.

Kaufman, Herbert. *The Forest Ranger: A Study in Administrative Behavior.* Baltimore: Johns Hopkins University Press, 1960.

Keen, Peter G. W. "Implementation Research in OR/MS and MIS: Description versus Prescription." Graduate School of Business, Stanford University, 1977, working paper no. 390.

Kotter, John P. *Organizational Dynamics: Diagnosis and Intervention.*

Leavitt, H. T. *et al. New Perspectives in Organization Research.* New York: Wiley, 1964.

Leonard, Frank S. "Management Assumptions: the Underlying Structure for Behavior in the United States Forest Service." Unpublished doctoral dissertation, Harvard University, Graduate School Business Administration, 1978.

Litecky, Charles and Gray, Jack. "A Model of Systems Analysis, Design, and Control." Minneapolis: Management Information Systems Research Center, University of Minnesota, 1974, MISRC-WP-74-02.

Lucas, H. C. "Behavioral Factors in System Implementation." Stanford University, Graduate School of Business, 1973, Research paper no. 188.

———. *Why Information Systems Fail.* New York: Columbia University Press, 1975.

McKenney, James L. "A Field Research Study on Organizational Learning." Graduate School of Business Administration, Harvard University, 1978.

———. "Avoiding Organizational Obsolescence." Graduate School of Business Administration, Harvard University, 1978.

———and Gremillion, L. L. "Managing the Organizational Learning Process in Implementing Computer-Based Systems." Harvard University, Graduate School of Business Administration, 1978, working paper no. 78-32.

———et al. "An Analysis of Fiscal Year 1979 Program Planning in the U. S. Forest Service." Graduate School of Business Administration, Harvard University, working paper no. 78-15.

Narasimham, Ram and Schroeder, Roger. "An Empirical Investigation of Implementation as a Change Process." Minneapolis: Management Information Systems Research Center, University of Minnesota, 1976, MISRC-WP-76-11.

Nolan, Richard L.; McFarlan, F. Warren; and Norton, David P. "A Framework for Information Systems Development." In *Information Systems Administration*. New York: Holt, Rinehart and Winston, 1973, pp. 5–13.

Odiorne, George S. *Training by Objectives: An Economic Approach to Management Training*. London: Collier-MacMillan, 1970.

Oliver, Paul. "Examining Programming Costs." *Computer Decisions* 10:4 (April 1978): 51.

Orlicky, Joseph. *The Successful Computer System*. New York: McGraw-Hill, 1969.

Robinson, Glen O. *The Forest Service: A Study in Public Land Management*. Baltimore: The Johns Hopkins University Press, 1975.

Rubenstein, Albert H. *et al.* "Some Organizational Factors Related to the Effectiveness of Management Science Groups in Industry." *Management Science* 13:8.

Schlaifer, Robert. *User's Guide to the AQD Collection*. Boston: Harvard Business School, 1977.

Schultz, Randall L. and Slevin, Dennis P. *Implementing Operations Research/Management Science*. New York: American Elsevier Publishing, 1975.

Singer, Edwin J. *Training in Industry and Commerce*. London: Institute of Personnel Management, 1977.

Tracey, William R. *Evaluating Training and Development Systems*. New York: American Management Association, 1968.

Trist, E. L. "On Sociotechnical Systems." In *The Planning of Change*. Bennis, Warren G. *et al* (eds.). New York: Holt, Rinehart and Winston, 1976.

USDA Forest Service. *Land Areas of the National Forest System*, 1978.

———. *Orientation to the Forest Service*. Draft Copy, 1976.

USDA. *Early Days in the Forest Service*. Missoula: U. S. Forest Service Northern Region, 1943.

Upton, Molly. "Price Performance Shift Seen Continuing." *Computerworld* 11:39 (August 1977): ?.

Weyerheuser Corporation. *Weyerheuser Approach to Uniform System Implementation*. Tacoma: Weyerheuser, 1970.

Whitelaw, Matt. *Evaluation of Management Training: A Review*. London: Institute of Personnel Management, 1972.

Zaleznik, Abraham; Christiansen, C. R.; and Roethlisberger, F. J. *The Motivation, Productivity, and Satisfaction of Workers, A Prediction Study*. Boston: Harvard University Division of Research, 1958.

Index